PLAY, SPORT, AND SPIRIT

PLAY, SPORT, AND SPIRIT

Patrick Kelly, SJ

Paulist Press
New York / Mahwah, NJ

Cover images by: *top row, left and right* KeithJJ/Pixabay.com, *center* Alexander Nadrilyanski / Pexels.com; *bottom row, left to right:* Anastasia Shuraeva / Pexels.com, football wife Pexels.com, and IMG_1979/Pexels.com
Cover design by Joe Gallagher
Book design by Lynn Else

Copyright © 2023 by Patrick Kelly, SJ

All rights reserved. No part of this publication may be reproduced, stored in a retrieval system, or transmitted in any form or by any means, electronic, mechanical, photocopying, recording, scanning, or otherwise, without either the prior written permission of the Publisher, or authorization through payment of the appropriate per-copy fee to the Copyright Clearance Center, Inc., www.copyright.com. Requests to the Publisher for permission should be addressed to the Permissions Department, Paulist Press, permissions@paulistpress.com.

Library of Congress Cataloging-in-Publication Data
Names: Kelly, Patrick M. (Patrick Michael), 1960- author.
Title: Play, sport, and spirit / Patrick Kelly, SJ.
Description: New York/Mahwah, NJ : Paulist Press, [2023] | Includes index. | Summary: "This book illuminates the human and spiritual meaning of sport and work"—Provided by publisher.
Identifiers: LCCN 2022040350 (print) | LCCN 2022040351 (ebook) | ISBN 9780809156443 (paperback) | ISBN 9780809188055 (ebook)
Subjects: LCSH: Play—Religious aspects—Christianity. | Work—Religious aspects—Christianity.
Classification: LCC BT709 .K35 2023 (print) | LCC BT709 (ebook) | DDC 233/.5—dc23/eng/20230111
LC record available at https://lccn.loc.gov/2022040350
LC ebook record available at https://lccn.loc.gov/2022040351

ISBN 978-0-8091-5644-3 (paperback)
ISBN 978-0-8091-8805-5 (e-book)

Published by Paulist Press
997 Macarthur Boulevard
Mahwah, New Jersey 07430
www.paulistpress.com

Printed and bound in the
United States of America

For Mihaly Csikszentmihalyi
in gratitude for your goodness,
gentleness, and generosity and for the way
you used your considerable gifts to help
improve the quality of human life

No honest game is entirely lacking in the capacity to instruct. I think that this delightful exercise with the ball represents a significant philosophy for us.

Cardinal Nicholas of Cusa, 1450

Play should interest our contemporary world more than perhaps it does. Not only in the United States, but all over the world [people] today [are] much concerned with freedom, and the world of play is the world of freedom itself—of activity for its own sake, of spontaneity, of pure realization. Today, however, we seldom associate freedom with play. Freedom is grim—something to be fought for, something that we feel may confront us with antagonisms and even hatred instead of generating effusiveness and spontaneity and joy.

Walter Ong, SJ, 1967

CONTENTS

Preface ix

Acknowledgments xix

Chapter 1. What Is Sport? 1

Chapter 2. Play and Sport: Historical and
　　　Theological Considerations I 19

Chapter 3. Play and Sport: Historical and
　　　Theological Considerations II 43

Chapter 4. The Evolution of Play and Sport 61

Chapter 5. The Freedom of Playing Sports 71

Chapter 6. The Joy of Playing Sports 101

Conclusion 125

Notes 133

Index 169

PREFACE

I ALWAYS ENJOYED PLAYING SPORTS. As a boy I would spend hours on end throwing the ball against the wall and catching it with my baseball glove, shooting baskets, or playing games with other kids. The hours would go by in what seemed like minutes. I later played football and basketball for our high school teams and football in college. I can see in retrospect that throwing the ball against the wall or shooting baskets as a boy were akin to meditation for me. Sports also provided a context for me to reflect on life and its meaning. I kept a journal in high school of poems and spiritual reflections our coaches gave us related to sports or life in general. And I made close friendships with the teammates I played with in high school through college, some of which have lasted until this day. While in college, after having had some impactful spiritual experiences, I began to have a new interest in learning about the Catholic faith I had been raised in, as well as other religious traditions. I ended up going to the Jesuit-run University of Detroit for a fifth year of school and taking all theology and religious studies classes. I was happier that year than I had ever been in my life. A big part of the reason is that I met the Jesuits for the first time, and I was studying with them. This was the beginning of what would later become my Jesuit vocation. But that would still take several more years to become clear to me.

During my twenties, while teaching and doing graduate studies, I continued to play pickup basketball and coached some at high school and college levels. However, there was a part of me that felt that I should "put aside childish things," as St. Paul says. That is, that I should forget all about my playing days as a youth and get "serious" about living the Christian life. I realized over time, however, that this approach didn't work well for me. I understand now that this is because my participation in sport had too profoundly shaped me, both in good and not-so-good ways. And the human formation that took place while playing sports was affecting my attempts to live the Christian life in the present. It was not so easy to put the past behind me after all.

I can see in retrospect that there was an implicit dualism in my approach then. I was beginning to frame things as though my young, embodied life playing sports, with all its passion and joy, disappointment and hurt, didn't have anything to do with "life in the Spirit." As though I had two lives. It was only when I did the thirty-day Spiritual Exercises retreat as a Jesuit novice that this unconscious dualism was challenged in a profound enough way to initiate a conversion in my way of thinking. Fr. Gary Wright, SJ, my novice director, noticed that my youth and experiences playing sports kept coming up in our conversations and even during the retreat itself. And so, he encouraged me to let them enter my prayer on the retreat. As the retreat continued it became clear I was being invited to stay in touch with all those very human experiences I had as a young person playing sports. Eventually, when I was praying with the story of Jesus's baptism, I experienced a sense of a call to also walk with others who are engaged in this domain of culture.

As my Jesuit life has gone on, I have become increasingly convinced that play and sports are worthy of our attention. One summer as I was directing retreats at Wernersville retreat center in Pennsylvania, I came across Johan Huizinga's book *Homo Ludens: A Study of the Play Element in Culture*.[1]

Preface

Huizinga wrote about play in ancient and medieval societies and showed its profound significance for understanding culture and domains of culture as well as its connection to ritual and experiences of the sacred. I experienced this book as something of a revelation. It felt like a whole new world was opening up to me intellectually; but at the same time what I was reading about was intimately connected to *my* world, the world of play I had always inhabited and with which I was most familiar.

Later in my Jesuit training, when I was teaching a class on sports, education, and religion at the University of Detroit Mercy, a Jesuit friend introduced me to psychologist Mihaly Csikszentmihalyi's book *Flow: The Psychology of Optimal Experience*.[2] In Csikszentmihalyi's writings I read for the first time a scholarly account of what the experiences I had all my life playing sports *felt like*. Early in his academic career, Csikszentmihalyi wanted to understand why play was enjoyable. To help him in this endeavor, he studied people involved in various forms of play and other autotelic activities. The word *autotelic* comes from the two Greek words *auto* (self) and *telos* (goal, purpose, end). An autotelic activity, then, has its goal or purpose in itself.

I could easily relate to the elements of flow people experienced during various play—and some work—activities: centering of attention, merging of action and awareness, egolessness, union with one's surroundings, effortlessness, the transformation of time. Csikszentmihalyi mentioned in his earliest publications that people also have experiences analogous to flow in creative endeavors and "in contexts usually called 'transcendental' or 'religious,'" including in collective ritual, the practice of Zen, Yoga, and other forms of meditation, or "practically any other form of religious experience."[3] One of the things that intrigued me were similarities I noticed between the flow experience and the way Ignatius of Loyola described "spiritual consolation," which I had been learning about in my Jesuit formation.[4] It was a great privilege to be able to do my doctoral studies with Professor Csikszentmihalyi and afterward to have him as a mentor and friend until his untimely death in 2021. I have dedicated this book to him in gratitude for his influence on me personally and on my vocation as a scholar.

But I've gotten ahead of myself. What is needed first for U.S. culture, before getting to spiritual or religious traditions, is an account of what sport is and its human and cultural significance. If we don't have such an account, sport remains vulnerable to being valued only as a means to external goods, such as money and fame. Even viewing sport primarily as a means to character development can cause problems, if it bypasses basic questions about what sport is and its internal goods and intrinsic rewards. Indeed, it is only by giving a "thick description" of sport and its internal goods and intrinsic rewards that we can begin to understand its spiritual significance from the perspective of religious traditions. With this approach we can also more precisely identify when and how sport is being corrupted, given that what is being corrupted are sport's internal goods or intrinsic rewards. Of course, when we begin to reflect on what sport is and its human and cultural significance, this leads us into the territory of play.

I have written elsewhere that in some of the earlier cultural and theological traditions of the West, play is accepted as a part of life and even taken seriously intellectually.[5] For example, thirteenth-century theologian Thomas Aquinas asked in his *Summa Theologica*, "Can there be a virtue about games?" His answer? "Yes." Aquinas followed Aristotle and other ancients who understood moderation as central to virtue. For him, working or being serious all the time would be immoderate; therefore, a person also needed to have play and recreation in his or her life.

Preface

For Aquinas, then, play is an important part of a fully human life. Ethical problems arise only from play's misuse or from having too much or too little of it. One's play could be harmful to others or indecent, for example. People might play too much or at the wrong times (e.g., when they should be at Mass) or in the wrong places (e.g., in burial yards). But, as was alluded to, for Aquinas it is also possible to sin by having too little play in one's life. As he puts it:

> In human affairs whatever is against reason is a sin. Now it is against reason for a [person] to be burdensome to others, by offering no pleasure to others, and by hindering their enjoyment. Wherefore Seneca says: *Let your conduct be guided by wisdom so that no one will think you rude, or despise you as a cad.*[6]

In some earlier writings Aquinas pointed out that sometimes people play so that they can, for example, return more refreshed to their studies. In his *Summa Theologica* and other writings, however, he emphasizes that play is engaged in for its own sake (i.e., is "autotelic"). Indeed, for Aquinas play was like contemplation because they both were enjoyable and engaged in for their own sake. As someone influenced by Aristotle, however, he thought that every virtuous act was directed to an end. He raised the objection to his own position that if play is done for its own sake (i.e., not for an end), how can it be virtuous? His response is that the enjoyment we experience in play *is* directed to an end: the good of the player. As he put it, "Actions done [playfully (*actiones ludicrae*)] are not directed to any external end; but merely to the good of the [player], in so far as they afford him pleasure or relaxation."[7] In other words, the end of play has to do with the human person experiencing life to the full.

PLAY, SPORT, AND SPIRIT

Aquinas's "play ethic" was the most important influence on late medieval preaching related to play and sport.[8] This play ethic also influenced the Renaissance humanists and the early Jesuits, providing them with the rationale for including play and sport in their schools. Indeed, this ethic still influenced Catholic immigrants to the United States in the nineteenth century. This influence is evident in the reasons they gave for including play and sport in Catholic schools and in the joyful—and at times, raucous—way students themselves described their experiences playing sports during the school day.[9]

Aquinas's insight that play is engaged in for its own sake yet benefits the player serves as a starting point for the considerations in this book. I am trying to understand in our context how sport, experienced as play and engaged in for its own sake, can also have benefits for players and contribute to their flourishing. While I am making use of insights from Aquinas as a starting point—and think that the cultural and theological traditions of the later medieval and early modern periods have something to offer our current reflections on sport—I am not calling for a simple return to these periods or ways of thinking. Such a return is impossible, in any case. Rather, we need to think these issues through in light of our contemporary understandings of the human person.

This book is situated in the emerging academic discipline of Catholic spirituality, with an emphasis on the spirituality of Ignatius of Loyola. Having said that, I hope the book is of interest and accessible to readers from other religious traditions or to those who are not affiliated with any religious tradition. Huizinga points out that play is older than culture (because animals play), but it is also a human universal. In this sense, it is something everyone can relate to. I have tried to keep the focus on peoples' lived experiences of play as these have occurred historically and in our contemporary context. When I don my

Preface

hat as a Catholic theologian, my approach has been to enter into a genuine dialogue with Protestant theologians about play. I would invite persons from other religious traditions to bring elements of their own religious/spiritual heritage into dialogue with what they are reading as well. And, on a personal level, I would encourage you to "take what you need and leave the rest," as they say at twelve-step meetings. In the courses I teach, we study Zen meditation, the Confucian and Taoist notion of *wu-wei*, and other religious/spiritual traditions in relation to the material in this book. I have also published about sport in relation to these traditions (see n. 4). But due to time and space considerations, I have limited myself in this book to bringing the experiential dimension of play and sport into dialogue with Catholic and Ignatian theological and spiritual traditions.

Scholars in the discipline of spirituality study *lived experience*, which is complex and multifaceted. To understand lived experience in all its richness and complexity, it is helpful to study it using the lenses of different academic disciplines. Thus, scholars of spirituality go about their work in an interdisciplinary way. They choose a discipline, or disciplines, that will be most helpful with respect to the *question* they are addressing. As was mentioned, my question is "How can sport, experienced as play and engaged in for its own sake, also have benefits for players and contribute to their flourishing?"

In chapter 1, I write about how play has been marginalized in sport and even in youth sport in recent decades in the United States. I then draw on the research of Johan Huizinga to help us understand what play is and how it is related to culture, ritual, festival, and spirituality, and to make an initial case for understanding sport as play. In chapter 2, I show how sport—as lay Catholics experienced it in the high and late medieval and early modern periods up through the nineteenth century in the United States—manifested the characteristics of play described by Huizinga. The experience of Protestants in the early colonies and until the nineteenth century in the United States was different from that of Catholics. The Puritans emphasized that godliness was connected to work and tended to regard play with a new level of suspicion. They eliminated all feast days, on which their ancestors in England and other parts of Europe had regularly played games and sports for centuries. They outlawed or at least frowned upon play on the Sabbath as well. The emergence of a capitalist economy and industrialization further encouraged the emphasis on work. In this context, one of the main concerns of prominent Protestant ministers in the mid-to-late nineteenth century was the marginalization of play in sport and in U.S. culture. They argued passionately for the need to include time and space for play in the Christian life.

In chapter 3, I write about how in the late nineteenth and twentieth centuries important Catholic and (later) Protestant theologians, drawing on earlier theological traditions, wrote profound books about the human and spiritual significance of play. But they didn't direct their attention in any sustained way to sport itself. And no other theologians were making use of their writings to reflect on sport either. Their rich reflections on play, then, did not influence sport as an aspect of U.S. culture. Later, Protestant theologians and other scholars wrote about various ways Protestant cultural, theological-ascetical traditions and sport interacted. Religious studies scholars wrote a good deal about sport as a civil or folk religion. These theologians and scholars did not focus their attention on the play element of sport, however. It is only more recently, with the advent of what Michael Sandel calls a "market society" and the increasing instrumentalization of sport, including youth sport, that both Catholic and Protestant theologians have begun to turn their attention explicitly to this topic.[10] This is an opportune time (a *kairos*), then, for an in-depth consideration of how the experience of *playing* sport has benefits for players and is related to their experiencing life to the full.

In chapters 4 through 6, I draw on psychologist Gordon Burghardt's scholarship on play in the context of evolution,[11] Randolph Feezell's philosophical reflection on the freedom of play in sports,[12] and psychologist Mihaly Csikszentmihalyi's research on the flow experience in sports.[13] These scholars help us understand in our contemporary context how the experience of sport, as play engaged in for its own sake, benefits players and contributes to their human flourishing. Because there is a "through line" between the experiences of play described by these scholars and the lived experiences of the Christian life as described by Ignatius of Loyola and other spiritual writers, their research can also help us to gain new insights into the relationships between play, sport, and spirituality.

While there is much in our cultural and even theological/spiritual heritages in the United States that tends to set play and work in opposition, these scholars do not accept the view that there is an unbridgeable gap between play and work. My own discovery, as I have been trying to understand the human and spiritual significance of play and sport with the help of their research, is that play has much to teach us about how we can become more fully human in and through our work as well. Such reflection needs to be taking place in Catholic theology, which regards the human being as the purpose of work.[14] According to John Paul II's encyclical "On Human Work," each person is a subject capable of deciding about him or herself, and "with a tendency to self-realization." Through the process of work itself, he or she "becomes 'more a human being.'"[15] This book will help us to understand how this happens in light of new insights into what it means to be human gleaned from the interdisciplinary study of play.

ACKNOWLEDGMENTS

I am very grateful to Brian McDermott, SJ, Richard Baumann, SJ, Randolph Feezell, Nicholas Austin, SJ, Amy Bauer, and Justin Kelly, SJ, all of whom read part of the manuscript and provided me with helpful feedback, corrections, and advice. A special thanks to Daniel Dombrowski and Simon Hendry, SJ, who read the entire manuscript and provided helpful feedback as well. Thanks to Catherine Smith for patient and careful editing. And it has been a pleasure to work once again with Donna Crilly, my editor at Paulist Press.

Chapter One
WHAT IS SPORT?

> Is there still an area of human action, or human existence as such, that does not have its justification by being part of the machinery of a "five year plan"? Is there or is there not something of that kind?[1]
>
> *Josef Pieper,* Leisure: The Basis of Culture

WHAT IS SPORT? Is it an industry? Is it "war minus the shooting," as George Orwell has remarked?[2] Or is it to be understood as a kind of play? It matters a great deal how one answers this question. By naming something we shape our perception of it. From this perception all sorts of practical and theoretical consequences follow. The way we name things is influenced by all sorts of factors having to do with the culture we live in and its assumptions, value orientations, and blind spots. I will say more about some of these later, but for now suffice it to say that the commonly held view that sport is an industry—which has been shaping academic programs and research agendas in universities in the United States for some time now—may reveal more about our particular context as a capitalist and consumer society than it does about the activities that we usually call by the name of sport as these have been experienced in diverse historical and cultural contexts. When we use war as a primary metaphor for sport in Orwell's sense, this may tell us more about the modern world in which the quest to win in sport can become deadly serious because winning is tied to a sense of personal worth and external goods such as money and fame, than it does about some essence of the activity itself.

In my own thinking about this question, I have been influenced by the philosopher Randolph Feezell. Feezell doesn't try to identify an unchangeable nature or essence of sport. Rather, he says that if we consider sport as a kind of play, following play theorists such as Johan Huizinga and Roger Callois, it "strikingly [reveals] the relevant phenomena" in a more adequate manner than other accounts.[3] I agree with him on this point, and I will say more about this later.

I think it makes sense to consider sport as a kind of play in part because of my own experiences playing sports as a child and on school teams from fourth grade through university. I played because it was fun. This doesn't make me unique, as many studies confirm that this is the top reason young people give for participating in sports.[4] However, in my experience there were dynamics even in high school that could have turned sport into something else. I played high school football and basketball in the highest division of a very competitive Catholic league in Detroit, Michigan. I remember our football coach insisted that when we took leave of one another we say, "Work hard," rather than our usual "Take it easy." (It was the 1970s and the rock band the Eagles had just put out a hit song by the latter name.) Even though school sports did require a lot of effort and a significant investment of time, I was willing to put all of this in because it was so much fun. It seemed that most of my friends were playing for the same reason. For me, this is what made playing sports worthwhile, and I still think this was the most important aspect of the experience today.

Playing football in college was less enjoyable. Training was year-round and more specialized. Whereas in high school I had played several positions (as well as other sports), in college I just played free safety. At times it seemed like I was spending my whole life backpedaling, as I was doing drills associated with playing defensive back year-round. Because we had a very good team, as free safety I was not involved very much in running plays during games (the tackles were made earlier), so even games became somewhat boring. I did return punts in college, which lessened the boredom somewhat. We were highly successful, won conference championships, and went to the national playoffs in our division. I was a team captain, All-Conference free safety, and one of the leading punt returners in the nation (Div. II). However, something that had been at the heart of my motivation for playing football was beginning to disappear.

In our contemporary context, sports are not always playful. All one needs to do is visit a Little League baseball game and watch the parents' behavior to confirm this fact. Many parents and coaches today encourage children to specialize in one sport at an early age and then train year-round. The motivation for early specialization on the part of parents and coaches is to give the young people an "edge" over others—in the race for college scholarships or, for the big dreamers, a professional contract. Such early specialization has been related to a dramatic rise in overuse injuries in youth sports; children's bodies are not mature enough to bear year-round training in a single sport.[5] Bruce Ward, the director of physical education and athletics in San Diego's public schools, is concerned that year-round intensive training causes young people to lose touch with the joy of playing their sport. "The shame of it is you see how hardened these 14-year-olds are by the time they get to high school....They're talented, terrific players, but I don't see the joy. They look tired. They've played so much year-round, they are like little professionals."[6]

These dynamics are also influenced by the trend toward privatization of youth sport and the financial interests of those who run for-profit club teams. According to sociologist Jay Coakley,

> Many parents don't realize that the current emphasis on early specialization in youth sports is due in great part to the privatization and professionalization of youth sports. When sport clubs, both non-profit and commercial, hire staff and coaches, there needs to be a way of ensuring that payrolls, facility costs, and other expenses can be paid twelve months a year. The only way this can be done is to convince parents that year-round participation is in the best interests of their children, and that dues must be paid every month of the year. But this approach is grounded in the logic of economic profit, and it has nothing to do with the best interests of children.[7]

This approach is leading many young people who train seriously year-round in one sport to experience burnout and even to stop playing their sport. The increased seriousness in youth sport is also leading many other young people, who aren't looking for a scholarship or to play at an elite level, to drop out of organized sport by the age of thirteen. Since the top reason young people give for playing sports is that it is fun, it shouldn't surprise us that the number one reason they give for dropping out is that it is no longer fun.[8] Also, the coupling of youth sport with the "pay to play" system means that children from poorer families and communities increasingly cannot afford to play.[9]

If even youth sport is no longer playful, it should not be surprising that sport at higher levels often does not manifest the play element either. The seemingly endless parade of athletes who have been caught using performance enhancing drugs, including Marion Jones, Alex Rodriguez, and Lance Armstrong, is clear evidence of this fact. Given that winning at elite and professional levels is tied to the acquisition of money, status, and power, the attitude that "winning is the only thing" has become widespread. Such attitudes are not limited to individuals. The state-sponsored doping of athletes by Russia at the 2012 Olympic Games in Sochi was also fueled by the desire for external goods, that is, confirmation of an ideological system and international hegemony. Cheating can also be found in youth sports. For example, a U.S. Little League championship team and some successful high school athletic programs have attained their success by using ineligible players.[10]

But what I have been describing has to do with the *corruption* of sport. Many social theorists, starting with the Marxist school, but also those influenced by Michel Foucault and others, have become so taken with the corruption in sport, that this is all they tend to see. They typically don't acknowledge that there exists anything apart from the corrupting dynamics.[11] And so, they tend not to ask the obvious question: If the current dynamic is corrupting, what is it that is being corrupted? And in what precisely lies the corruption?[12] To answer such questions, we must have some understanding of what sport is and its human and cultural significance. This is why I am drawn to the work of scholars like Randolph Feezell and Mihaly Csikszentmihalyi, whose writings attempt to understand what sport is and its internal goods or intrinsic rewards.

PLAY, SPORT, AND SPIRIT

If sport is understood under the category of play, then one way to understand the corruption of sport today has to do with the increasing marginalization of the play element. In this sense, sport suffers from the same problems as many other domains of culture that are increasingly valued only in relation to external goods such as money, prestige, and status. Our context has raised for us the curious question about whether there are activities that have internal goods or intrinsic meaning anymore—that are worth doing for their own sake. To say that sport is a kind of play is to give an affirmative answer to this question.[13]

HUIZINGA ON PLAY

To understand sport as play it is first necessary to understand what play is. The most obvious place to begin our consideration of play is with the writings of Johan Huizinga, whose book *Homo Ludens: A Study of the Play Element in Culture* put play on the map for scholars in several disciplines.[14] Huizinga pointed out that at the time he was writing, scholars had not yet studied play in its own right. When they did turn their attention to play, they tended to focus on its usefulness for other purposes. Some scholars had shown that play discharges excessive vital energy or satisfies an imitative instinct; some had pointed to the role that play has in training a young animal for the serious work of adult life; still others had explored other ways play serves ends outside of itself.[15] To each of the above explanations of play, Huizinga wrote, it might be objected,

> So far, so good, but what actually is the *fun* of playing? Why does the baby crow with pleasure? Why does the gambler lose himself in his passion? Why is a huge crowd roused to frenzy by a football match?

What Is Sport?

> This intensity of, and absorption in, play finds no explanation in biological analysis. Yet in this intensity, this absorption, this power of maddening, lies the very essence, the primordial quality of play.[16]

For Huizinga, the fun of playing tends to resist analysis and logical interpretation. It can't be reduced, as a concept, to any other mental category. "Nevertheless," he writes, "it is precisely this fun-element that characterizes the essence of play."[17]

In contrast to the approaches he criticizes, Huizinga focuses on the experience of play itself and what it means for the player. "We shall try to take play as the player himself takes it," he wrote, "in its primary significance."[18] Huizinga's attention to the experience of play itself makes his research very important for scholars of spirituality—and for this book. As mentioned in the introduction, scholars of spirituality study *lived experience*. And they use different academic disciplines to do so. With his training in linguistics and research as a cultural historian, Johan Huizinga offers us very important insights into the experience of play. Because scholars of spirituality have not paid much attention to play, his research will make a significant contribution to the academic discipline of spirituality.[19]

One reason Huizinga's research is so important is that he helps us to see that we cannot understand play adequately only in relation to work—and negatively, at that. This has been a predominant way of understanding play in the United States, which is rooted in religious conceptions. The Puritans exercised significant influence in this regard. Following John Calvin, they associated godliness with one's calling or work. They regarded play with such suspicion because it distracted people from steady application to their work.[20] Influential Puritan theologian Richard Baxter expressed this view in his *Christian Directory*, where he lamented that his readers have no mind of your work, because your mind is so much upon your play....[You] are weary of your business, because your sports withdraw your hearts....[They] [play and sports] utterly unfit you, and corrupt your hearts with such a kind of sensual delight, as makes them more backward to all that is good.[21]

This attitude also explains the Puritan opposition to the feast days that populated the medieval calendar. Later, Puritan attitudes toward work and play influenced other Protestants in the United States. In the nineteenth century, the editors of the Congregationalist magazine *The New Englander* wrote,

Let our readers, one and all, remember that we were sent into this world, not for sport and amusement, but for *labor*; not to enjoy and please ourselves, but to serve and glorify God, and be useful to our fellow men. This is the great object and end of life.... In pursuing this end, God has indeed permitted us all needful diversion and recreation....But the great end of life after all is *work*.[22]

In the above quotations, work and play are described in opposition to each other. According to anthropologist Victor Turner and other scholars, this was a change from premodern societies where work and play were hardly distinguishable in the performance of rituals and festivals, for example. For Turner, our own clear distinction between work and play is one of the artifacts of the Industrial Revolution that was fueled by the Protestant work ethic. In this context, "'work' is understood as the realm of the rational adaptation of means to ends, of 'objectivity,' while 'play' is thought of as divorced from this essentially 'objective' realm," and as "its inverse, as 'subjective.'"[23]

Because we have tended to regard play with suspicion—and even associated it with sin—the play element in sport has been easier to marginalize in the United States than it would have been otherwise. The seeming naturalness with which we view sport merely as a means to external goods, such as college scholarships, money, prestige, or institutional advancement, arose in the context of this longer heritage.[24] Over the last forty years the situation has become more acute, however. During this time Michael Sandel argues that we have entered an era of market triumphalism and have drifted "from *having* a market economy to *being* a market society." For him, a market society is "a way of life in which market values seep into every aspect of human endeavor. It's a place where social relations are made over in the image of the market." For Sandel, it is not by chance that the era of market triumphalism coincided with "a time when public discourse has been largely empty of moral and spiritual substance." And this is unfortunate, because in order to understand where markets belong and where they don't in sport and other areas, we have to deliberate "about the meaning and purpose of goods, and the values that should govern them."[25]

PLAY, SPORT, AND CULTURE

If play cannot be adequately understood only negatively in relation to work, is there a better way of understanding it? For Huizinga, play is older than culture. He says this is obvious because many animals play and they "have not waited for man to teach them their playing."[26] In his view, all the essentials of human play are present in the play of other animals. For example, they enjoy themselves, keep to rules that indicate that this is not "ordinary life" (you shall not bite hard on your playmate's ear), invite one another with ceremonial gestures, and are fully immersed in what they are doing.

For Huizinga, while play is older than culture, it is fundamental to all human cultures. He complains about the tendency of people (including the editor of his book *Homo Ludens: The Study of the Play Element in Culture*) to change the title of his talks and writings to "the play element *in* culture" from his own preferred "the play element *of* culture." While the first version suggests that play was one element in culture among others, the latter version more accurately expresses his intention "to ascertain how far culture itself bears the character of play."[27] As he put it in *Homo Ludens*:

> The view we take in the following pages is that culture arises in the form of play, that it is played from the very beginning....By this we do not mean that play turns into culture, rather that in its earliest phases culture has the play-character, that it proceeds in the shape and mood of play. In the twin union of play and culture, play is primary.[28]

I will say more about how Huizinga understands the relationship between play and aspects of culture such as festival and ritual later in this chapter. For now, let us consider what play itself is. Huizinga sums up the formal characteristics of play as follows:

> [Play is] a free activity standing quite consciously outside "ordinary" life as being "not serious," but at the same time absorbing the player intensely and utterly. It is an activity connected with no material

interest, and no profit can be gained by it. It proceeds within its own boundaries of time and space according to fixed rules and in an orderly manner.[29]

In another place he writes,

> Play is a voluntary activity or occupation executed within certain fixed limits of time and place, according to rules freely accepted but absolutely binding, having its aim in itself and accompanied by a feeling of tension, joy and the consciousness that it is "different" from "ordinary life."[30]

In Huizinga's view, the phenomena of play offered a challenge to the materialistic and mechanistic understandings of life and human existence that were common in biology, psychology, and other academic disciplines in his time. One could find numerous passages where he makes this point, including the following:

> However we may regard it, the very fact that play has a meaning implies a non-materialistic quality in the nature of the thing itself.
>
> [By] acknowledging play you acknowledge mind, for whatever else play is, it is not matter....Play only becomes possible, thinkable and understandable when an influx of *mind* breaks down the absolute determinism of the cosmos.
>
> The purposes [play] serves are external to immediate material interests or the individual satisfaction of biological needs. As a sacred activity play naturally

contributes to the well-being of the group, but in quite another way and by other means than the acquisition of the necessities of life.[31]

He provides historical examples from a variety of cultures to illustrate that human beings do not only live for the satisfaction of material wants and are not merely passively shaped by their environment. Although play is separate from "ordinary life," in the sense that it stands outside the immediate satisfaction of wants and appetites, and provides an interlude, as a "regularly recurring relaxation" it does become an integral part of life in societies. "It adorns life, amplifies it" and to that extent it is important for persons and society "by reason of the meaning it contains, its significance, its expressive value, its spiritual and social associations....It thus has its place in a sphere superior to the strictly biological processes of nutrition, reproduction and self-preservation."[32]

For Huizinga, the first and main characteristic of play is that "it is free, is in fact freedom." We voluntarily enter into it because it is fun; we do it for its own sake. While playing we are not trying to satisfy immediate needs and wants, either. As he puts it, "In play there is something 'at play' which transcends the immediate needs of life and imparts meaning to the action."[33] In this sense, we have some detachment from what we usually tend to think "makes the world go round," things like money, prestige, or power. Even though play isn't associated with the serious matters of ordinary life, it is characterized by complete immersion and absorption in the activity.

We don't have to play; it is unnecessary. Think of the baseball diamond or basketball court in the middle of your school campus or city. These don't have to be there for a school or a city to be what they are; they are gratuitous. (This is easy to understand with respect to schools, given that many schools

What Is Sport?

in countries other than the United States do not have such large, formal spaces for playing sport.) And yet we build these separate spaces for play and make up the sports we play in them as well as their constitutive rules.[34]

The constitutive rules help to separate our play from ordinary life. In his discussion of the role of such rules in games, Bernard Suits distinguishes between prelusory and lusory goals. One of the goals in golf, for example, is to put the golf ball into the cup. The easiest way to do this would be to walk up to the hole and drop the ball in with your hand. Viewed from a prelusory perspective, this would make sense. However, the rules do not allow it. They proscribe the most efficient way of reaching one's goal. Indeed, they introduce gratuitous challenges that make reaching the goal more difficult. The players must start, say, 350 yards from the hole and hit the ball with a golf club. Between the tee and the hole may be placed creeks, ponds, and sand traps. The fairway may bend and the green tilt in one direction. The lusory goal has to do with hitting the golf ball into the cup with these and other challenges added.

For Suits, when players accept the constitutive rules just because they make playing the game possible, they engage with a "lusory attitude." The constitutive rules help to create "another world to live in" temporarily that is different from ordinary life—where we usually opt for the most efficient ways to reach our goals. According to Huizinga, the rules of our games are so important because they "determine what 'holds' in the temporary world circumscribed by play....Indeed, as soon as the rules are transgressed the whole play-world collapses. The game is over."[35]

The experience of entering into "another world" is also facilitated by the fact that sports are played in a place and time set apart. In sports, the physical boundaries of the court, playing field, pool, and so on are clearly defined; the actions that take place within them have meaning in relation to the constitutive rules. Sports like baseball allow us to step out of ordinary time temporarily into a more leisurely mode, as the dynamics of the game itself determine how long it will last. For sports like basketball where time is kept, the time that comes to matter is on the scoreboard (say, 2:30 left in the game), rather than "ordinary time" as measured by our watches, phones, and the like (say, 9:32 p.m. on a Tuesday night). The way we experience time subjectively is different when we are playing as well. Most often, when we are immersed in playing a sport "time flies" and hours can go by in what seems like minutes. On the other hand, sometimes time seems to slow down if the player needs it to in order to do something well (think of a batter in baseball trying to hit a 96-mph pitch that is changing directions).

PLAY, RITUAL, AND THE SACRED

According to Huizinga rituals are also a form of play. One reason he gives for this is their "spatial separation" from ordinary life. For him, both the playground and the "consecrated spot" for rituals "are temporary worlds within the ordinary world, dedicated to the performance of an act apart." They transport participants to "another world."[36]

Rituals in the premodern societies that Huizinga was primarily writing about in *Homo Ludens* were religious in nature. For him, this didn't remove them from the play category, however. On the contrary, he thought that the sacred rituals of ancient societies were performed "in a spirit of pure play truly understood."[37] He quotes Plato, for example, who in his *Laws* writes that "God alone is worthy of supreme seriousness."

> But man is God's plaything, and that is the best part of him. Therefore every man and woman should live life accordingly, and play the noblest games and be of another mind from what they are at present.... What, then, is the right way of living? Life must be lived as play, playing certain games, making sacrifices, singing and dancing, and then a man will be able to propitiate the gods, and defend himself against his enemies, and win in the contest.[38]

Human beings participate in rituals throughout the year, but these are especially important during festivals, which themselves constitute a hallowed time, when "ordinary life is at a standstill." Karl Kerényi pointed out that scientists and other scholars had not taken feasts seriously. Indeed, as he put it, "for all science is concerned it [the phenomenon of the feast] might not exist at all." "Neither might play, we would like to add," Huizinga commented.[39] For Huizinga, the fact that scientists and other scholars neglected *both* festival and play was understandable, given that they share their main characteristics in common.

> In the very nature of things the relationship between feast and play is very close. Both proclaim a standstill to ordinary life. In both mirth and joy dominate, though not necessarily—for the feast too can be serious; both are limited as to time and place; both combine strict rules with genuine freedom.[40]

For Robert Bellah, several features of play—the fact that it has internal goods, is delimited in time and space, has

PLAY, SPORT, AND SPIRIT

norms or rules, requires cooperation, shared intentionality, and attention—lead him to concur with Huizinga that ritual is a form of play. Indeed, for him "ritual is the primordial form of serious play in human evolutionary history."[41] And in his view, religion "grows out of the implications of ritual in a variety of ways that never leave ritual entirely behind."[42]

Huizinga discusses the chapter "The Playfulness of the Liturgy" from Catholic theologian Romano Guardini's *The Spirit of the Liturgy* to make the case that ritual is a kind of play. Guardini points out that it is possible to regard any object, reality, or activity with respect to either its purpose or its meaning. Purpose has to do with an end that the thing in question serves outside of itself. Yet, he points out that "no phenomenon can be entirely, and many can be, to a minor degree only, comprehended in this category." He asks, for example, what is the use of the "extravagance of shapes, colors, and scents in Nature? To what purpose the multiplicity of species? Things could be so much more simple."[43]

> Measured by the standard of apparent and external utility, there is a great deal in Nature which is only partially, and nothing which is wholly and entirely, intended for a purpose, or, better still, purpose*ful*. Indeed, considered in this light, a great deal is purposeless.[44]

Regarding such phenomena in nature, but also every created reality, he says it is helpful to shift our angle of vision from purpose to *meaning* if we are to understand them more adequately. The standpoint of meaning looks to the phenomenon in itself. For Guardini, objects that have no purpose in the strict sense can have a meaning, which consists in their being what they are. "Measured by the strict sense of the word, they are purposeless, but still full of meaning." The meaning of each created thing is that it should exist and reflect something of the glory of God who created it. And the meaning of each living being is "that it should live, bring forth its essence, and bloom as a natural manifestation of the living God."[45]

This is the context within which he understands liturgy as a kind of play. As he puts it, liturgy has in common with the play of children and the life of art that "it has no purpose, but it is full of profound meaning." Indeed, for him, participation in the liturgy helps people "not to see purposes everywhere."[46]

> The soul must learn to abandon, at least in prayer, the restlessness of purposeful activity; it must learn to waste time for the sake of God, and to be prepared for the sacred game with sayings and thoughts and gestures, without always immediately asking "why?" and "wherefore?" It must learn not to be continually yearning to do something, to attack something, to accomplish something useful, but to play the divinely ordained game of the liturgy in liberty and beauty and holy joy before God.[47]

Now that we have some understanding of what play is and its relationship to sport, culture, festival, and ritual, in the next two chapters we will consider more explicitly the relationship between play and sport from the late medieval period in Europe to the present day in the United States. The understanding of this relationship has historically been profoundly influenced by theological and spiritual sensibilities and continues to be to this day.

Chapter Two

PLAY AND SPORT

Historical and Theological Considerations I

We now come to speak of the sports of the city, for it is not fitting that a city should be merely useful and serious-minded, unless it also be also pleasant and cheerful.[1]

William fitz Stephen,
"Description of London" (12th c.)

THE UNDERSTANDING OF SPORT as play makes a good deal of sense when considering sport in late medieval and early modern Europe. For one thing, in those societies people participated in games and sports on feast days and Sundays. It is significant that the feast days took up more than one-third of the year (varying in frequency depending on the period and region). Natalie Zemon Davis lists some of the activities found "in all the cities of France, and indeed of Europe" from the later medieval period through the sixteenth century:

PLAY, SPORT, AND SPIRIT

> Dancing, music-making, the lighting of fires; reciting of poetry, gaming, and athletic contests—the list in all its forms and variations would be longer than the 81 games in Bruegel's famous painting or the 217 games that Rabelais gave to Gargantua. They took place at regular intervals, and whenever the occasion warranted it; they were timed to the calendar of religion and season (the twelve days of Christmas, the days before Lent, early May, Pentecost, the feast of Saint Jean Baptiste in June, the Feast of the Assumption in mid-August, and All Saints) and timed also to domestic events, marriages, and other family affairs.[2]

Davis points out that, aside from the feast of fools, which was sponsored by clerics, "virtually all the popular recreations were initiated by laymen."[3]

As I mentioned in the last chapter, the relationship between feast days and play is very close. During feast days and while at play, "ordinary life is at a standstill."[4] According to Huizinga, on these days, people participated in rituals and dramas that themselves can be understood as forms of play. To the extent that the feast days, with their rituals, initiated people into an experience of a loving and faithful God, they provided a "relaxed field" (about which more later) in which people could engage in gratuitous activities unrelated to the serious concerns of "ordinary time." Being "betwixt and between" the structures and hierarchies of ordinary life and their roles within these, people could also experience a "relatively undifferentiated comitatus, community, or even communion of equal individuals."[5]

Play and Sport I

THEOLOGIANS OF PLAY

Some of the most influential theologians during these periods also reflected on play and its place in the Christian life. As was mentioned in the preface to this volume, in his *Summa Theologica*, Thomas Aquinas asks the question, "Can there be a virtue about games [*ludi*]?" Because he follows Aristotle in understanding virtue to be associated with moderation, he answers in the affirmative. If a person spent the whole of his or her life working or preoccupied by it, this would be excessive. As he puts it:

> *I pray thee, spare thyself at times: for it becomes a wise man sometimes to relax the high pressure of his attention to work* [Augustine]. Now this relaxation of the mind from work consists in playful words or deeds. Therefore it becomes a wise and virtuous man [*sic*] to have recourse to such things at times. Moreover the Philosopher assigns to games the virtue of eutrapelia, which we may call *pleasantness*.[6]

Aquinas understands play as a natural part of human life and societies. And he supported the profession of actors and comedians. He points out that play is needed for the intercourse of human life because it provides pleasure and recreation to people weary from too much work. For this reason, it may have a legitimate occupation associated with it. "Wherefore the occupation of play-actors, the object of which is to cheer the heart of man, is not unlawful in itself."[7] It is only if comedians or actors misuse their acting, for example by being indecent or causing harm to others, or if they introduce acting into undue matters or seasons, that their behavior would be unethical. In response to the objection that comedians or actors direct their whole life to acting and are therefore excessive, Aquinas says that their work is not the whole of their lives. He points out that in addition to their work they may also pray, moderate their passions, and help the poor.

For Aquinas, play was also important for people in religious life and for the secular clergy. Indeed, he thought because they were engaged in contemplation and with matters of the soul, which could be even more tiring than other kinds of work, recreation was crucial for their health and well-being. He records a story from the Church Fathers in this regard:

> In the *Conferences of the Fathers* it is related of Blessed John the Evangelist, that when some people were scandalized on finding him playing together with his disciples, he is said to have told one of them who carried a bow to shoot an arrow. And when the latter had done this several times, he asked him whether he could do it indefinitely, and the man answered that if he continued doing it, the bow would break. Whence the Blessed John drew the inference that in like manner [a person]'s mind would break if its tension were never relaxed.[8]

According to Aquinas, there can be sin in a lack of play. For him, this would be the case if a person is always serious or working and eschews all fun and relaxing activities. As he puts it:

> In human affairs whatever is against reason is a sin. Now it is against reason for a man to be burdensome

to others, by offering no pleasure to others, and by hindering their enjoyment. Wherefore Seneca says: Let your conduct be guided by wisdom so that no one will think you rude, or despise you as a cad.[9]

In the *Summa Contra Gentiles*, Aquinas writes that play activities are sometimes engaged in for their own sake, and sometimes for the sake of an end, as when we play to relax our minds so we can study better afterward.[10] In his more mature reflections in the *Summa Theologica* and elsewhere, however, he emphasizes that play activities are engaged in for their own sake. "Playful actions themselves considered in their species are not directed to an end," he writes.[11] He takes up the objection that play engaged in for its own sake cannot be virtuous, because virtuous acts must be directed toward an end. He responds to the objection by saying that it is true that play is not directed to an external end (such as money or fame), but that the enjoyment of play is directed to the "recreation and rest of the soul." He says in another context that "actions done [playfully (*actiones ludicrae*)] are not directed to any external end; but merely to the good of the [player], in so far as they afford him pleasure or relaxation."[12] And the fulfilled good (*bonum consummatum*) of the player is his ultimate end.

If, as Aquinas says, while we play we are not pursuing external ends, we are often pursuing internal goods. And in other parts of the *Summa*, he points out that we experience delight at play when we attain a good that we seek. For him, "just as good is desired for itself, so delight is desired for itself and not for anything else."[13] However, regarding what he calls the formal or motive cause, delight is desired by reason of the good, "which is the object of that delight, and consequently is its principle, and gives it its form: for the reason that delight is desired is that it is rest in the thing desired."[14]

In sport, this is played out as we desire to attain the internal goods of our sport; when we attain these we experience delight, as something of a side effect. Both attaining the good and the concomitant delight are intrinsically rewarding.[15]

According to Aquinas, we experience something analogous to this dynamic in our relationship with God. For him, happiness is the attainment of, or resting in God, our final end. And he argues that "delight is necessary for happiness. For it is caused by the appetite being at rest in the good attained. Wherefore, since happiness is nothing else but the attainment of the Sovereign Good, it cannot be without concomitant delight."[16] As Josef Pieper puts it, for Aquinas every delight is "consequent to a good" and there also is a delight "consequent to that which is in itself the supreme good."[17]

Aquinas's way of framing things helps us to understand how our experiences of play and other autotelic activities can be included in our movement toward our last end. In such cases the good of the person, which is experienced as he pursues the internal goods of an activity and experiences a concomitant delight, is part of his human formation that will prepare him to recognize and appreciate analogous dynamics in his experiences of contemplation. They will feel familiar. In this regard Thomas says that what is true for play is true for speculative science, which is also "sought for its own sake." Responding to the criticism that science, therefore, is not desired for the last end, he says that what he said about play "applies to speculative science[,] which is desired as the scientist's good, included in the complete and perfect good, which is the ultimate end."[18]

This does not mean that the person who is playing needs to be explicitly thinking about God, his last end, at every moment. Indeed, this wouldn't seem to be possible, given the deep immersion in the activity itself that is experienced while at play. The same principle would apply to other kinds of activities, such as teaching or scientific research, that typically involve deep concentration on the task at hand and full immersion in what we are doing. "One need not always be thinking of the last end," Thomas writes, "whenever one desires or does something." What is key is our "first intention," which is of God, which "remains in every desire directed to any object whatever, even though one's thoughts be not actually directed to the last end. Thus while walking along the road one needs not to be thinking of the end at every step."[19]

But Aquinas goes even further than this regarding the significance of play for the Christian life. In a commentary on a text from Ecclesiasticus, he describes contemplation itself as a kind of play. The text from Ecclesiasticus reads, "Run ahead into your house and gather yourself there and play there and pursue your thoughts." In contemplation, Aquinas writes that

> it is...necessary that we ourselves should be fully present there, concentrating in such a way that our aim is not diverted to other matters. Accordingly, the text goes on, "And gather yourself there," that is, draw together your whole intention. And when our interior house is entirely emptied like this and we are fully present there in our intention, the text tells us what we should do: "And play there."[20]

He says that contemplation is "suitably compared" to play in the above passage because of two features of play.

> First, we enjoy playing, and there is the greatest enjoyment of all to be had in the contemplation of wisdom. As Wisdom says in Ecclesiasticus 24:27, "My spirit is sweeter than honey."

Secondly, playing has no purpose beyond itself; what we do in play is done for its own sake. And the same applies to the pleasure of wisdom....The contemplation of wisdom contains within itself the cause of its own enjoyment, and so it is not exposed to the kind of anxiety that goes with waiting for something which we lack. This is why it says in Wisdom 8:16, "Her company is without bitterness" (the company of wisdom, that is) "and there is no boredom in living with her." It is for this reason that divine Wisdom compares her enjoyment to playing in Proverbs 8:30, "I enjoyed myself every single day, playing before him."[21]

Thomas Aquinas's "play ethic" was one of the most important influences on preaching about play and sport on feast days in the late medieval period.[22]

HUMANIST AND EARLY JESUIT SCHOOLS

Aquinas's "play ethic" also influenced the thinking of the humanists of the Renaissance and the early Jesuits regarding how to organize the school day and year for their students. Their writings emphasized that their students should not be studying all the time because it would be excessive; students also needed time for recreation and play. Aeneas Piccolomini, who later became Pope Pius II, wrote in a treatise about education for the still very young King Ladislaus:

> I approve of and praise your playing ball with boys your own age....There is the hoop; there are other

perfectl[y]
ers shou[ld]
ation and
not alway[s]
nor shoul[d]
may be cru[...]

The early J[esuits...]
and time for play[...]
buildings that wer[e...]
opened in the late s[...]
selves, however, in[...]
play games and spo[rts...]
after lunch and in be[...] very
Thursday. In the wa[...] would walk to the
Jesuit villa on recreat[ion d]ays with some of the younger Jesuits
in formation and play games there.

The Jesuits had continued the medieval practice of observing the feast days and the holy days of the church year. In the academic context, feast days were observed with a vacation day from school. Occasionally, in the course of a week the students would have two vacation days: the recreation day just mentioned and a feast day (depending on when the feast day fell). These free days were occasions for the students to play various games and sports. The Jesuits also scheduled longer vacations for the students at Christmas, Easter, and in the summer months.[24]

Detailed instructions regarding recreation in the schools and vacation days would soon be articulated in the *Ratio Studiorum* of 1599, the formal education program for the Society's schools. "A nice balance should be maintained," the authors of the *Ratio* wrote, "between study time and recreation periods."[25] Because the *Ratio* was the plan of studies for all Jesuit schools, it became common to set aside time for recreation and sports

...PIRIT

...ols in Europe and other parts

...ury French Jesuit François Pierron ... more broadly to his reflections on life ... said would be somber and boring without ...ation. "Recreations are called such," he wrote ...*recepteur*, "because they give new being to spir-... are overwhelmed by too much work."²⁷ For Pierron, ... should not continue without ceasing, and if a person has ...tended to their responsibilities, "it is very reasonable that one would enjoy some rest from time to time, and that one would take some recreation."²⁸

CATHOLICS IN THE "NEW WORLD"

Many of the French Jesuit missionaries in North America had attended Jesuit secondary schools in France and so would have been familiar with play and sport being accepted as a part of life. They would have also been introduced, in their philosophy and theology studies, to Thomas Aquinas's "play ethic." These influences are evident in their basic stance of acceptance and appreciation of Native American games and sports. Josef Lafitau, SJ, wrote in the very first lines of the chapter entitled "Games" in his book *Customs of the American Indians Compared with the Customs of Primitive Times*:

> Besides the necessary occupations the Indians have others which are either pure diversion, as are their games of chance, or diversion mixed with exercise, which are in the province of gymnastics, serving to exercise and form the body. These games are among

Play and Sport I

the first institutions of men, and the first with which the ancient authors have acquainted us.[29]

The journals of Jesuit missionaries contain many matter-of-fact descriptions of the games they observed while living with the Native Americans. Fr. Paul du Ru observed a kind of ball game among the Muskogeans in Mississippi, for example:

> We walked to the village where there were games and a great dance. The men play in pairs; one of them has a ball in his hand and throws it ahead. Both of them run as fast as they can, throwing a big stick after this ball and, as well as I could make out, the one whose stick is closest to the ball wins the play. Then the one who wins throws the ball the next time. This is a rather strenuous game: nevertheless, it is played by both old and young.[30]

The women also played ball games. As Fr. du Ru commented, the women

> separate into two parties between two large posts in the square. Somebody throws a little ball in the center, and the one who seizes it first tries her best to run around the post on her side three times, but she is prevented by the women of the opposite party who seize her if they can. When she can no longer resist them, she throws the ball to her people who make a similar effort to run around their post....The games are very long and ordinarily when they are over the women plunge into the water to refresh themselves. Sometimes the men play this game also.[31]

PLAY, SPORT, AND SPIRIT

Catholics also incorporated play and sport into their schools in the United States as a matter of course. From the time Georgetown College opened in the late eighteenth century, play and sport were advertised and promoted as dimensions of student life. A 1798 public advertisement for the "College of George-Town" stated that the school was dedicated to "the improvement of youth in the three important branches of *Physical*, *Moral*, and *Literary* education."[32] In 1809, the school's advertisement pointed out that "the garden and court adjoining, where the young gentlemen play, are very airy and spacious. The situation is very pleasant and healthy."[33] According to Joseph Durkin, from the earliest years at Georgetown

> dinner was followed by "recreation" or playtime for an hour and a half. Spacious playing fields were available. The popular sports were handball, a rudimentary kind of football that was probably more like present-day soccer, and gymnastic exercises. Fencing and boxing also had their devotees.[34]

Even a cursory reading of the students' articles about the annual Field Days in the *Georgetown College Journal* in the nineteenth century makes it clear that the sports on these days were a time for enjoyment and fun. They were also a time to poke fun at classmates. In 1878 the student author "D.U." tells his readers about the hurdles, in which

> Chew made a graceful finish in the unprecedented time of one second, but unfortunately he made it at the very first hurdle, which proved to be his *pons asinorum*, and over which he executed a double somersault which would have kindled enthusiasm in the heart of the average showman.[35]

Play and Sport I

Because it was clear who was going to finish first and second in the race, all the excitement centered in "who should bear off the honors of the rear." It looked like Walsh might do so, but he made a sudden spurt and shot by other runners. His flight was a short one, however:

> On one of the last hurdles, he was observed to fall like a shooting star, and strike a graceful and becoming attitude upon his head. Whether he assumed this position in the wild exhilaration of the moment, or whether he was forced to it by the attraction of gravity, we cannot say.[36]

In the tug of war, one of the Lawler brothers on one end would from time to time turn completely around and put the rope over his shoulder and move forward,

> damaging to a great extent the efforts of Conde Palle just next to him who being considerably smaller in stature, was sometimes observed dangling in mid-air, while at other times, the sudden depression of the rope would reveal him in a sitting posture, whence the elevation would again relieve him, making his whole performance look something like that of a puppet worked by means of a string. McManus [meanwhile] pulled with steady earnestness, his face exhibiting that expression of intense agony mingled with hope often to be seen in representations of the early Christian martyrs.[37]

In D.U.'s description of the greased pig race, during which students tried to catch a pig that had been let loose in the field, he tells his readers how the pig ended up stuck among cartwheels and stumps and other objects. "Then, in our efforts to disentangle him, he would suddenly rush at us with a perfect crescendo of squeals, attempting an occasional nib at our calves in a way not altogether conducive to social feeling."

> The pig disappeared in the crowd, but soon emerged dragging little Henry Touceda after it at a wondrous rate of speed, so that a grave doubt arose in our minds whether Henry had the pig, or the pig had Henry. But as the prize was awarded to the boy, and as the pig was not even mentioned as second, we can confidently assert that Henry won the race.[38]

In 1843, the program of studies that president Fr. Edward Sorin, CSC, outlined for University of Notre Dame students alternated between study and recreation as well. Dr. Thomas Low Nichols, a doctor on his way from Detroit to Chicago, stopped at Notre Dame's campus in the 1850s and saw what he described as a "scene that filled me with admiration." Along with a Gothic church, clusters of buildings and two lakelets, he mentions seeing "a large playground, with gymnastic apparatus."[39] A great distance in another direction he saw "a crowd of boys at play in the college-grounds; a group of them was bathing in a secluded cove of one of the lakes, watched by a man in a long black robe." He describes how the hour of recreation had been sounded on a bell and "study, devotion, and work were laid aside" as students, teachers, priests, and nuns "enjoyed their hour of innocent and sometimes boisterous mirth." After the midday meal one could hear the "glad hurrahs" of the students in the playgrounds while the teachers and priests enjoyed "the leisure after-dinner hour."[40]

In 1864, the Notre Dame community took part in a feast day celebration to honor Fr. Edward Sorin's patron, St. Edward.

Play and Sport I

After dinner, the entire community, with distinguished guests from Chicago, went to a large meadow to watch and "partake in some good olden time field sports."

> The games commenced with foot races. Next followed "sack races." Then came "Wheel-barrow races." Ten boys, with eyes blindfolded, ran a hundred and fifty yards, each wheeling a barrow; and the first who entered the goal received the prize. Next came the grand divertissement of the day—a pig chase! A wild, lank and earless pig was turned loose in the meadow and twenty of the swiftest runners chased him, and he who caught him and held by its "narrative" was to receive the pig as his reward. The sports ended with a "grinning match." Tired and sore, some from exercise, others from excessive laughter, but all pleased and happy, the sportsmen returned to the University.[41]

The school schedule at Villanova, the Augustinian university near Philadelphia, also alternated between study, recreation, and sport. Thomas C. Middleton, an Augustinian friar, wrote about the sports and games that were played at the school when he was a student in the 1850s. He pointed out that every Thursday was a free day and "sports of some kind or other filled the interval between breakfast and supper." On Sundays there were no games in the morning, so churchgoers were undisturbed. "But Sunday afternoons, Vesper hour excepted, were given over to the full and free to suit the spirit of joyousness in whatever exercises the students chose to pass their leisure."[42]

According to Middleton, students at Villanova regularly engaged in walking, hunting, swimming, and skating. Ball games were plentiful: handball, pot ball, shinny (something like hockey), town ball (the ancestor of baseball), football (in a Celtic style), and "number all" (akin to baseball).

> Other favorite games were Hop, Step and a Jump; Hank-a-dea, Prisoner's Base, Duck-on-Davy, and Tag. Foot races, too, were among the tricks of speed, besides many sorts of jumping games, such as: vaulting with pole, high jump, as well as broad and long. One of the prefects, afterwards priest, was for many years the college champion, with twenty-two feet to his credit.[43]

According to Middleton, "Everybody, it seemed, liked to take part in our pastimes; seniors or juniors, professors or students, were alike welcomed to come into any game."[44]

NINETEENTH-CENTURY DISSIDENT PROTESTANTS ON PLAY[45]

Congregationalist pastor Washington Gladden painted a very different picture of attitudes toward sport in Protestant contexts in his 1866 *Amusements: Their Uses and Abuses; A Sermon*. As he reflected on his childhood, he lamented the fact that his own Christian upbringing had led him to think that playing sports was sinful; or that if he did play them, he should do so with the utmost seriousness. As he put it,

> In my boyhood I used to think that if I became a Christian it would be wrong for me to play ball; or if I engaged in the sport I must do so in a serious

Play and Sport I

and thoughtful way, with none of the hilarity and abandon which made the ball-ground so attractive to me. If I had become a Christian then I am sure I should have felt bound to repress all my boyish exuberance of spirits, and my conscience would have reproached me for engaging in any pastime which gave it vent. Yet doubtless the boyishness that was in me would have proved stronger than those mistaken convictions of duty, and I should have presented the common, though somewhat paradoxical spectacle of a human being committing sin in doing that which is perfectly right.[46]

Gladden questioned the suspicion of enjoyment of play and sports that the Puritans had bequeathed to the Protestant churches, and he noted that this was not the doctrine of the New Testament. He pointed to Jesus himself who signaled his entrance to public ministry by "mingling in the festivities of a wedding." In his view

it ought to be a part of the religious instruction of the young that sport, glee, fun, not the dismal, repressed, shame-faced variety, but the real hilarious, exuberant sort, is their lawful inheritance; and that there is by divine appointment, "a time to laugh," as truly as a time to pray. Then their consciences will not be constantly tormented with the thought that it is wicked to do that which they are all the while longing to do.[47]

Gladden argued for a more holistic approach to the Christian life that would make room for the "hilarity and abandon" of the ball-ground. He comments that no person "is able to keep his faculties constantly in working tension. They must be

PLAY, SPORT, AND SPIRIT

relaxed occasionally, not only in rest, but also in play. Amusement is therefore as much a part of the divine economy as prayer, and one can glorify God by play, as well as by work or by worship."[48]

Since many Protestants in the nineteenth century regarded young people playing sports with suspicion, it is not surprising that they took an even dimmer view of adult play. Unitarian minister Edward Everett Hale wrote in his 1855 essay, "Public Amusement for Poor and Rich," that according to the prevailing norms a person of "business character" was not expected to do anything so frivolous as to play. "I am afraid it would be thought a severe strain on business character," he wrote, "if it was whispered that a bank director, or a member of the board of aldermen, or a young lawyer, or a judge, were seen playing in a game of cricket, or joining in a rowing match of an afternoon. If they indulge in such levities at all, it must be before sunrise, or after sunset."[49]

According to Hale, even the few holidays that Americans celebrated were hardly occasions for rejoicing or play. As he put it,

> I have been hoping, since I was a boy, that some man would arise, of power…in shewing poor, haggard New England, how to amuse herself. He has never come, and she does not know how. You see, every year, throngs of people who have come into town to spend "Independence Day," sadly pacing hand in hand up the streets and down again, unamused, unrejoicing,—wishing that the holiday were over, before it has half gone by. I have wished that some man of intellectual power as severe as Goethe's,… would appear, to shew our hard-workers how to rest themselves,—our hard-thinkers how to play. That

man has never come, and those workers do not know how.⁵⁰

While he was pastor (1833–1859) of the North Congregational Church of Hartford, Connecticut, Horace Bushnell wrote the book *Christian Nurture*, which focused on how Christian parents should raise their children. Bushnell felt that too great an emphasis on sin and the depravity of the person apart from salvation in Christ made it difficult for Protestants to recognize God's presence in the life of their children. He points out that a common way of thinking among Protestants at the time says, "My child is a sinner…; and how can I expect him to begin a right life until God gives him a new heart?" He countered this way of thinking with the reminder that God is present at each moment of our lives, including in our childhood years. What is more appropriate to the doctrine of spiritual influence itself, he asks

> than to believe that as the Spirit of Jehovah fills all the worlds of matter, and holds a presence of power and government in all objects, so all human souls, the infantile as well as the adult, have a nurture of the Spirit appropriate to their age and wants? What opinion is more essentially monstrous, in fact, than that which regards the Holy Spirit as having no agency in the immature souls of children who are growing up, helpless and unconscious, into the perils of time?[51]

For Bushnell, play provides children with an experience that can help them to understand the liberty that God's grace brings about in the Christian life. Indeed, for him,

> play is the symbol and interpreter of liberty, that is, Christian liberty; and no one could ever sufficiently

conceive the state of free impulse and the joy there is in it, save by means of this unconstrained, always pleasurable activity, that we call the play of children. Play wants no motive but play; and so true goodness, when it is ripe in the soul and is become a complete inspiration there, will ask no motive but to be good. Therefore God has purposely set the beginning of the natural life in a mood that foreshadows the last and highest chapter of immortal character.[52]

Bushnell also thought feast days and holidays were very important for young people. And he thought this was true of religious festivals, especially Thanksgiving and Christmas. For him, both are festivals of gratitude: Thanksgiving for the blessings of Providence, and Christmas for the way Providence has given the world a Savior and salvation. Such festivals will help children understand that religion is not only about "dry restraint."

> For nothing will go farther to remove the annoyance of a continual, unsparing, dry restraint upon the soul of childhood, and produce a feeling, as respects religion, of its really genial character, than to have it bring its festive and joyously commemorative days.[53]

On these religious holidays he felt that children should have the opportunity to play freely. And he recommended vigorous physical play that takes place outdoors: "Those plays are generally to be most favored that are to be had only in the open air, and in forms of exercise that give sprightliness and robustness to the body."[54]

Play and Sport I

In an 1897 article entitled "The Problem of Amusement," sociologist W. E. B. Du Bois wrote about the attitudes of African American Christians toward amusements and recreation. He provided historical and social context for his reflections by pointing out that "every vestige" of the primary sociological group that was the family "among the Negro slaves was destroyed by the slave ship." This meant that in the United States "the first distinct voluntary organization of Negroes was the Negro church." In the later nineteenth century, the church had become the center of the people's "social, intellectual and religious life."[55] This development meant that if the people were going to have amusements and recreation, these would also take place in the context of the church.

According to Du Bois, the approach to amusements and recreation in African American churches had been heavily influenced by Baptist and Methodist theological sensibilities, which tended to lead to a "wholesale condemnation," an "undue repression."[56] And he was afraid that

> proverbially joyous people like the American Negroes are forgetting to recognize for their children the God-given right to play; to recognize that there is a perfectly natural and legitimate demand for amusement on the part of the young people, and that no people can afford to laugh at, sneer at, or forcibly repress the natural joyousness and pleasure-seeking propensity of young womanhood and young manhood.[57]

Du Bois points out that after the church, the next most important social institution was the school. And he was concerned that there was a bias against play in schools that educated Black children as well.

PLAY, SPORT, AND SPIRIT

In these schools of primary grade especial attention should be paid to athletic sports; boys and girls should be encouraged to run, jump, walk, row, swim, throw and vault. The school picnic with a long walk over hill and dale and a romp under the trees in close communion with Mother Nature is sadly needed. In fine, here should be developed a capacity for pure, open-hearted enjoyment of the beautiful world about us, and woe to the teacher who is so bigoted and empty-headed as to suggest to laughing hearts that play is not a divine institution which ever has and ever will go hand in hand with work.[58]

He writes that all life is rhythm. "The right swing of the pendulum makes the pointer go round, but the left swing must follow it;...the heart must beat and yet between each beat comes a pause." All throughout nature "we see one mighty law of work and rest, of activity and relaxation, of inspiration and amusement." For him, where the balance of work and recreation is best maintained is the best civilization. And those civilizations decline toward barbarism where work and drudgery are so predominate "as to destroy the very vigor which stands behind them" or, on the other hand, where relaxation and amusement become dissipation rather than recreation.[59]

Scholars of Protestant traditions and sport in the nineteenth century have written a good deal about what they call "Muscular Christians." The designation "muscular" itself tends to connote qualities such as manliness, health, patriotism, and morality. With respect to morality, scholars usually focus on the way muscular Christians saw sport to be *useful* for purposes of "character development" in intercollegiate settings in both the late nineteenth and early twentieth centuries.[60] And yet, when the Protestant authors we have considered—who

Play and Sport I

are sometimes considered "muscular Christians"—are read in the larger context of the religious and cultural history of the West, the marginalization of play stands out as central to their concerns. They argue that Christians need to value play more, including the "hilarity and abandon" associated with baseball and other sports, and make room to include such experiences in a more holistic approach to the Christian life.

Chapter Three

PLAY AND SPORT

Historical and Theological Considerations II

CATHOLIC THINKERS IN THE MODERN ERA

AS WE MOVED TOWARD the twentieth century, influential Catholic thinkers kept alive those theological and ethical traditions that we have been considering, which influenced attitudes toward play and sport.[1] Authors such as Cardinal John Henry Newman, Josef Pieper, and Walter Kerr were critical of the utilitarian philosophy and excessive work orientation of the modern world. They argued for the importance, in education, the arts, and sport, of pursuing internal goods for their own sake, the attainment of which results in delight. In *The Idea of a University*, Newman pointed out that there are "exercises of the body," such as those that took place in the *palaestra* or Olympic games of ancient Greece, that can be accounted as "liberal" whereas many intellectual exercises of his time would not be. As he put it,

> That alone is liberal knowledge which stands on its own pretensions, which is independent of sequel, expects no complement, refuses to be *informed* (as it is called) by any end, or absorbed into any art, in order duly to present itself to our contemplation. The most ordinary pursuits have this specific character, if they are self-sufficient and complete; the highest lose it, when they minister to something beyond them.[2]

His book is an extended argument that knowledge is not merely a "means to something beyond it…but an end sufficient to rest in and to pursue for its own sake." When approached in this way, the pursuit of knowledge in the university can be "sanctified to the service of religion." After all, he wrote, "we attain to heaven by using this world well…we perfect our nature, not by undoing it, but by adding to it what is more than nature, and directing it towards aims higher than its own."[3]

Jesuit Hugo Rahner's book *Man at Play* is the most extensive theological reflection on play by a Catholic writer in the twentieth century. He was inspired to take up this topic by Thomas Aquinas's passages on play discussed earlier. Although initially inspired by Aquinas, Rahner looks back to the Church Fathers (who were influenced by the ancient Greeks) and finds there rich resources for reflection about the playing of God, human beings, and the Church. He points out that Maximus the Confessor, commenting on the passage in Proverbs 8 about Wisdom "playing before the Father," worked out an "entire mystical theology of this playing of God." According to Rahner, Maximus's theology emphasized "that both creation and incarnation are expressions of God's love, and that this love, though full of meaning and purpose, is a love that works in creative freedom wholly ungoverned by necessity or constraint."[4] It is in this spirit, Rahner writes that we speak of the playing of God, who through this creative pouring out of himself makes it possible for the creature to understand him in the wonderful play of his works; who has made for us children's toys out of the bright and variegated forms of his world wherewith to educate us, his true paideia, for things unseen and eternal things which are real and earnest.[5]

Even the rigors of Cistercian monastic life don't squelch play. At least not according to Paul Quenon, who had been a novice under Thomas Merton. In his book *In Praise of the Useless Life* Quenon writes how, in a cultural context where it is common to assume that everything/everyone must be useful for something, in the monastery, "To live in gratitude simply for being becomes the motif of life, liturgy, and mutual love. It serves no apparent purpose, other than the hidden marvel of being in God. The meaning of love, according to St. Bernard, is love itself." For this reason, Quenon says life in the monastery "is radically a life of play."[6] Prayer follows the same pattern, according to Quenon. "Why should I pray? Basically it is for the sake of praying." It is true that prayer is for the world, for those in need, for the Church or individual people. "But unless it is rooted in the boundless freedom of love and confidence in God, it is void and crippled. It has some effect, perhaps, but lacks the current of grace and graciousness that flows from God."[7]

Former commissioner of Major League Baseball A. Bartlett Giamatti's reflections in *Take Time for Paradise: Americans and Their Games* are also situated in this broader philosophical and theological stream. While as an adult he seems to have rejected the Catholic faith of his childhood, he continues to make use of ideas from this heritage. He begins his reflections on sport with a discussion of leisure and writes about the close relationship for the Greeks between leisure, liberal education, and play. These were all understood to be autotelic activities, "that is, their goal is the full exercise of themselves, for their own sake, because in them a condition is achieved that is active, not idle; entertaining, not simply useful; perfecting of our humanity, not merely exploitative of it." The condition of freedom of spirit that is actively induced by these activities as a nourishment "simulates what is promised, or provided, by religious experience—a state of contemplation, vigorous and expansive....The result is to be careless, or carefree. It is to be happy."[8]

In his book *The Joy of Sports*, Michael Novak acknowledges the important contributions of several authors already mentioned regarding our understanding of play. In his view, "It is not surprising that Catholic writers, steeped in the pre-Calvinist era of the medieval festival, have been the first and most profound writers on play. Johan Huizinga's *Homo Ludens*, Josef Pieper's *Leisure, The Basis of Culture*, and Karl Rahner's *Man at Play* are the classics in the field." According to Novak, Catholics living in Latin, Mediterranean cultures never got on board with the excesses of the work orientation of the industrialized modern world. And they tended to be regarded by the proponents of such an orientation as "backward, lazy, hedonistic."[9]

Novak points out that Catholics differed from their Protestant counterparts in their way of understanding and valuing play. For Catholics, play is good in itself.

> Play lies outside the realm of *shoulds* and *musts*. Play is an expressive activity. It flows. It reveals outwardly the inner energies of the human being. One doesn't play *because* it is good to play. The natural activity of human beings *is* play....The proper category for play is not moral but natural.[10]

Play and Sport II

Protestants on the other hand, says Novak, tend to regard play as *important*, particularly for character development and preparing people for a useful life by instilling in them a work ethic. He notes that the title of his book, *The Joy of Sports*, when compared with the title of George Will's book about baseball, *Men at Work*, points to these differences between a Catholic and Protestant approach. In his view, a clear-headed lover of sport must oppose the cult of the "Christian athlete." The effort of those who promote such a cult "groans with Weighty Seriousness." Whereas, as Novak sees things, "sports are a delight because they are an aside....They are, deliciously, ends in themselves." Novak says he doesn't want to be unkind in his characterization of Protestant views, but that he is trying to "sound a distinctive note" in a Protestant culture.[11]

Novak describes well those attitudes toward play and sport in the United States that originated with the Puritans and subsequently influenced other Protestants and most Americans, (including, I would add, many Catholics). But, as we have seen, some influential Protestants in the nineteenth century pushed back against a "Weighty Seriousness" and made the case for more play in sport and in American life in general. They don't fit Novak's characterization of Protestants very well. And some contemporary Protestant theologians who are turning their attention to sport as play don't fit his characterization well either.

TWENTIETH-CENTURY PROTESTANTS ON PLAY

Concern about the marginalization of play in American culture, and in Protestant theology, continued as we moved into the twentieth century. In 1935, R. Worth Frank, Professor of

Philosophy of Religion and Christian Ethics at Presbyterian Theological Seminary, summed up the "dilemma" that Protestants faced in his time:

> Protestantism is in a dilemma as it faces the foregoing facts. On the one hand it proclaims a gospel of salvation which, it declares, is the sure and sole way to abundant life. On the other hand, it is without a philosophy of play in an age which knows that play is indispensable to an abundant life.[12]

Starting in the late 1960s, some Protestant thinkers began to develop a philosophy—and even a theology and spirituality—of play. In his 1969 book *A Rumor of Angels*, Peter Berger, sociologist of religion and Protestant theologian, wondered what an anthropological starting point would mean for doing theology. In this vein, he writes about play as one of several kinds of human experiences that serve as a "signal of transcendence." Following Huizinga, he points out that play is separate from ordinary life, has its own rules and way of experiencing the passage of time. For him, joy is play's intention. And the player apprehends joy as being "in some barely conceivable way, a joy forever." In this sense, the person who is playing is not only stepping from one way of marking time to another, "but from time into eternity."[13] It is this quality of play, he writes, that explains why it is associated with feelings of liberation and peace.

> The experience of joyful play is not something that must be sought on some mystical margin of existence. It can be readily found in the reality of ordinary life. Yet within this experienced reality it constitutes a signal of transcendence, because its intrinsic intention points beyond itself.[14]

Play and Sport II

In his 1969 book *The Feast of Fools*, Baptist theologian Harvey Cox lamented the marginalization of play in Western industrialized countries. He cites the disappearance in such countries of both the medieval feast of fools and festivals in general. Cox sounds more like Thomas Aquinas than Richard Baxter when he writes, "In my view, not only are prayer and play analogous but their kinship provides us with a sound contemporary access both to our religious tradition and to the future."[15]

> In our present world it is also crucial for the rich Western nations to recover something of their capacity for sympathetic imagination and noninstrumental *joie de vivre* if they are to keep in touch with the so-called "underdeveloped world." Otherwise, the rich Western nations will become increasingly static and provincial or they will try to inflict their worship of work on the rest of the world.[16]

German Lutheran theologian Jürgen Moltmann is similarly critical of the instrumentalist mindset and excessive work orientation that marginalizes play. In his 1972 book *Theology of Play*, he cites the Westminster Catechism of 1647, which asked the question "For what purpose has man been created?" The Catechism's answer is that we were created to glorify God and enjoy him forever. Moltmann points out that giving glory to God and rejoicing in God's existence and our own "by itself is meaningful enough."[17] This answer, he says, is different from the usual answers that focus on ethical goals and ideal purposes.

> When we ask, For what purpose do I exist? the answer does not lie in demonstrable purposes establishing my usefulness but in the acceptance of my existence as such and in what the Dutch biologist

and philosopher Buytendijk has called the "demonstrative value of being." Recognizing this, we escape the dreadful questions of existence: For what purpose am I here? Am I useful? Can I make myself useful?[18]

Moltmann refers to F. J. J. Buytendijk's research about the play of animals. For Buytendijk, the extravagant luxury we find in the world of living things, and nature's "purpose-free abundance," is what led biologists to the concept of self-representation. "To put it simply," Buytendijk wrote, "the birds are singing much more than Darwin permits."[19] Reflecting on human life in this context, Moltmann writes,

> Is not man's playful rejoicing in his existence, his pure unforced pleasure in creative play, and his fondness for expression and representation exactly that "demonstrative value of being" of which Buytendijk speaks in reference to animals? Then man's free self-representation has to be the human echo to the pleasure of God in his creation. The glorification of God lies in the demonstrative joy of existence.[20]

IMPACT OF CULTURAL, THEOLOGICAL TRADITIONS ON SPORT

Catholic cultural traditions and theological and ethical reflection about play were not a significant influence on sport in the wider American society during the nineteenth century and up through the 1960s. A part of the reason for this was anti-Catholic prejudice in the nineteenth and first half of the twentieth century. One way that Catholics dealt with such prejudice was to attempt to create essentially a separate society, of which schools were an important part. Through much of the nineteenth century, sports in Catholic schools were what today we would call "intramural" activities. They didn't bring lay Catholics or their cultural traditions with respect to sports into regular contact with the wider society.[21] Only in the latter part of the nineteenth and the early twentieth century did interscholastic competitions emerge. Contests between Catholic and public school teams began to attract widespread attention in some parts of the country. Many Catholics viewed these sporting competitions as an opportunity to show that they were as capable (that is, as strong, smart, resourceful, etc.) as Protestants and to claim a place for themselves in the wider society. This was done with remarkable success at many Catholic high schools around the country and at institutions of higher education such as the University of Notre Dame in Indiana and Immaculata College in Philadelphia, which had one of the country's earliest, and most successful, women's basketball teams. There was not much reflection, however, on what these sports contests were all about at a deeper level—or how they were related to Catholic beliefs or values. As time went on, Catholics assimilated to the dominant ethos in the United States; in the process they increasingly lost touch with the cultural as well as the theological and spiritual heritage described earlier. Most Catholics in the United States today are likely unaware of this heritage.

    While Catholic theologians did not embrace the Puritan work ethic, many Catholic theologians and pastors tended toward a moral rigorism, particularly around sexuality, as we entered the modern world. Charles Taylor sees such rigorism present in nineteenth-century France in a "disproportionate fuss" on the part of clergy regarding dancing and their attempts to suppress or clean up folk festivals. Young people who refused to change were denied communion. According to Taylor, the concern of priests with such matters seemed obsessive at times.[22]

Taylor also points out that the body/soul dualism of Descartes found its way into Catholic theology and spirituality in the modern period. Bodily engagement with the world was no longer regarded as the avenue to truth or to spiritual experience in the same way it had been in earlier periods. He refers to this as a process of "excarnation," by which he means "the steady disembodying of spiritual life, so that it is less and less carried in deeply meaningful bodily forms and lies more and more 'in the head.'"[23] Such "excarnation" is evident in a talk Pope Pius XII gave to the young men of Catholic Action in 1940. In this talk, the pope told the young men,

> Everything which has to do with physical exercise, with contests, rivalry, sport, interests and attracts the youth of today. But young Christians know that intellectual exercises and especially the race toward intellectual light…are all the more beautiful, noble, and gripping.[24]

Pius XII's words about the intellect being more important than physical exercises and sport are situated in a broader critique he is making of the modern world—which he condemns as "materialistic." But the unintended consequence of his approach is that it gives the impression that Christianity does not have to do with the body, but with the mind and soul. "You are seeking a mother who will teach you more the things of the mind and the spirit than those of the body and the material order," he told the young men. "And where have you found that mother and that most loving teacher? Where did she communicate to you, not the life of the body, but the life of the spirit, the most high destiny of your soul?"[25] In this way of framing things, the body appears to belong to the world, and the mind/soul to the church.

Pius XII emphasized the unity of the human person, body, soul, and spirit more in later talks and writings. Based on their view of the unity of the person, he and subsequent popes often commented on how participation in sport can foster human and even spiritual growth. They also applied the principles of Catholic social teaching to sport; they emphasized that the dignity of the human person should be the primary consideration when evaluating sport policies and practices, and the ways participation in sport can foster the common good and even the unity of the human family. Familiarity with these texts was lacking among Catholic theologians in the United States, however. Scarcely any theologians were referring to them or reflecting on sport as an aspect of American culture in light of them. Such efforts would not begin in earnest until the twenty-first century.

In addition, most of the important Catholic thinkers who kept alive the theological, ethical traditions associated with the "play ethic" (Newman, Pieper, Kerr, Rahner) were not writing about sport itself. And neither was anyone applying their reflections to sport in a sustained way. Huizinga considered sports and contests more generally as a kind of play, but he thought modern sport (he was writing in the 1930s) had completely lost its connection with play and, therefore, its cultural and spiritual significance. Huizinga was also a linguist and cultural historian and wasn't explicitly engaging play or sport from a theological perspective. Michael Novak's book, first published in 1967, articulates a Catholic "play ethic" of sport as distinct from a Protestant approach as we have seen, but this occurs in only one brief section of one chapter. More generally, Novak's "faith that seeks understanding" is a faith in sports. He is a believer in sports and is most interested in understanding sports as a kind of civil or natural religion.[26] Giammatti's *Take Time for Paradise*, first published in 1991, was the first book that drew on elements of the Catholic cultural and intellectual heritage to reflect on sport in a sustained way. His strained relationship with the church may be part of the reason that his reflections were not explicitly theological. It wasn't until the twenty-first century that Catholic theologians and scholars of spirituality began to recognize the importance of his reflections for their own work.

The stance of being "at war" with the modern world also caused problems with respect to our topic. In the wake of the Reformation, the emergence of a new scientific sensibility and the Enlightenment, and the French revolution, church leaders and many theologians tended to regard the religious, intellectual, and political developments associated with the modern world in thoroughly negative terms. In the nineteenth and early twentieth centuries, the popes published encyclicals focusing on the errors of the modern world and condemned both "modernism" and "Americanism."[27] Some Catholic theologians in the early to mid-twentieth century attempted to engage with the social, cultural, and intellectual movements or trends of the modern world, but they tended to run into trouble with church leadership. In the process a gulf was created between faith and cultural traditions. Pedro Arrupe, SJ, superior general of the Jesuits from 1965 until 1983, still saw this to be the case in 1978, when he wrote to Jesuits of an "abyss which separates faith and culture."[28] It is no surprise then that, as we entered the modern world, Catholic theologians and scholars had not been paying attention to the lived experiences of people in sport. It was precisely at this time that modern sport was beginning to have a new level of importance in many societies.

Dissident Protestant theologians who wrote about the importance of play in the nineteenth and early twentieth centuries were, likewise, swimming against a very strong current. The Puritan work ethic led to the elimination of virtually all feast days of the medieval calendar. And on Sunday, the one day free from labor, sports were either outlawed or frowned upon by many early in our country's history. Hard work was, in fact, needed to build the new republic. And the development of a capitalist economy and industrialization only accentuated the emphasis on work. The fact that factories powered by steam engines could operate around the clock extended working hours. It was difficult for their writings on play to gain a foothold in the face of such significant social trends and structural conditions, which also had their own religious or theological sanction.

Just as with Catholic writers, Protestant authors who wrote about play in the latter part of the twentieth century (Berger, Cox, Moltmann) were not writing in a sustained way about sport itself, and few applied their reflections on play to this area of culture. When scholarly works related to Protestant traditions and sport began to appear in more recent years, they focused on the "muscular" part of what came to be called muscular Christianity in England and America, Evangelical Protestant engagement with sport, or the influence of the Protestant work ethic on sport and recreation.[29] Religious studies scholars published a good deal about sport as a civil or folk religion.[30] These scholars did not write very much about the relationship between play and sport except for the occasional lament about the loss of the play element in sport. Sociologist Steven Overman pointed out, for example, that

> the bias of Protestant ethic societies is that play is justified if it can accomplish something....Play is expected to lead to positive consequences, whether promoting health or instilling serious carry-over values for success in life. There must be some worthy

end to justify participation in play activities. Given this requirement, it follows that much of American sport is concerned less with "playing the game" than with extrinsic goals such as making money, acquiring status, or carrying out a political agenda.[31]

In the second half of the twentieth century, popular groups such as the Fellowship of Christian Athletes and Athletes in Action, as well as some Protestant theologians, emphasized how sport can be helpful for character development or is an instrument that God has raised up that can be used to evangelize, but few were paying much attention to the experience of playing sport itself, before it is put to these uses. In the process they ran the risk of missing the meaning of the human experiences of sport. Ironically, this undermined their ability to understand how sport can form character and what the relationship is between sport and the "good news."[32]

THE CONTEMPORARY STATE OF PLAY

The coronavirus pandemic has provided those of us in the United States and around the world with a pause in our daily activities as well as our sports. People have had more time than usual to reflect on the meaning of our lives and the various activities we are engaged in. Over the last fifteen years or so Catholic and Protestant theologians and scholars of spirituality have also begun to reflect more explicitly and in dialogue with one another about the relationship between play and sport.[33] For these reasons, this is an opportune time (a *kairos*) to pivot and move in a new direction.

Play and Sport II

The recent volume *Sport and Christianity: Practices for the Twenty-First Century* is a good example of new collaboration among Catholic and Protestant theologians about the relationship between play and sport. In his foreword, Protestant sociologist Tony Campolo writes that while the theologies of the Puritans may have contributed to nurturing our becoming workaholics, this may be "one of few works that focuses on a Christian understanding of play."[34] And the editors write in their concluding chapter,

> One of the most prominent aspects of the book is the largesse of play—as the foundation of sport, as an element of worship, and as a primal human need. More than simply relief from the work-a-day world, play connects people to the Creator and to their humanity and can lift the human spirit beyond the mundane toward greatness and joy. It is this spirit of play that makes possible the spiritual practices that many athletes draw upon and which breathes life into their sporting practices.[35]

Indeed, among Protestant theologians there is now a lively debate about how to understand play and its significance in sports. Anglican priest Lincoln Harvey offers a corrective to the earlier noted Protestant approaches that focus on the usefulness of sport for building character or for evangelization. He emphasizes instead that sport is play, which is engaged in for its own sake. We freely engage in sport, which isn't necessary and yet is meaningful to us. Harvey connects this to the creation of the world and humanity, both of which are also "unnecessary, yet meaningful." "This would suggest that when we play—unnecessarily but meaningfully—we are living out

PLAY, SPORT, AND SPIRIT

our deepest identity as unnecessary but meaningful creatures. Simply put, we reverberate with ourselves. We chime with our being." This is the significance of sport, and Harvey doesn't think Christians should also be looking for potential benefits in the moral or spiritual life. Any move in this direction would be to instrumentalize sport. In his view, rather, sport "should... be left alone."[36] In contrasting sport with worship, he says that "sport is only for sport. It is the one thing that is not directed to the glory of God. That is what sets it apart."[37]

Robert Johnston disagrees. For him, play is autotelic and yet has benefits. And "it is this paradoxical reality that is at the heart of sport." He reflects on an experience he had at a screening of the movie *I Am Yup'ik* about a basketball tournament in Alaska for Yup'ik youth. The teenage star of the team, Byron Nicholai, was at the screening and he said he and his friends play basketball because they love it and because they are doing it together. Suicide is a major problem in the villages, and many of the homes are fatherless, and life is confusing for the teens. In this context, Nicholi said, "When I'm playing, I forget about all the problems I'm having. It makes me feel alive." Nathan Golon, one of the movie's directors, commented that "basketball is a way into other issues of cultural identity; basketball for the Yup'iks is more than just a sport."[38] Johnston comments on the paradox:

> Only when one is freely participating for the love of the game does it become actual play. But at the same time, these Yup'ik basketball games have meaning far beyond the court and game time. They reinforce relationships between the players, with their tribe, and with their surroundings; they revitalize the spirits of fans and players alike, who for the duration of the game, experience something of the wholeness of

Play and Sport II

life; and they produce long-lasting joy. There is…a value beyond the basketball court—sport has meaning "for family life, civic life, political life, work life" (and I might add, "spiritual life").[39]

Johnston's approach, which understands sport as autotelic, yet having benefits, is the same approach Thomas Aquinas takes to play, and is a helpful starting point for our considerations for this book. How are we to understand that it is possible to play sports for their own sake and yet also benefit from them as whole persons or even culturally? The next three chapters of this book are meant to help us answer that question. These chapters will draw on Gordon Burghardt's scholarship on play in the context of evolution, Randolph Feezell's philosophical reflection on the freedom of playing sports, and Mihaly Csikszentmihalyi's research on the flow experience in sports and its relationship to human flourishing. I will bring this contemporary scholarship into dialogue with resources from Catholic theological and spiritual traditions, which will help us understand how play, sport, and spirituality are related in our contemporary context. The new insights we gain about human beings and spirituality in our study of play and sport will also shed new light on the human and spiritual meaning of work and vocation.[40]

Chapter Four
THE EVOLUTION OF PLAY AND SPORT

> Play is a reality that we have not effectively confronted in science or society. Yet it may lie at the core of who we are and how we came to be.[1]
>
> *Gordon Burghardt,*
> The Genesis of Animal Play

IN THIS CHAPTER I WILL be drawing on the research of Gordon Burghardt, the author of numerous articles and the groundbreaking book *The Genesis of Animal Play: Testing the Limits*, which help us to understand play in an evolutionary context. In the article "Modeling Play: Distinguishing between Origins and Current Functions," Burghardt and his colleagues point out that the most common question researchers have when studying play is "Why do animals play?" And the "why" is usually considered in terms of the adaptive benefits that the animals gain from such behavior. However, "this represents only one of the possible 'why' questions that can be asked about a trait," the authors write.[2] Because "some forms of play, especially in its earliest appearance, may have no functional value," it is important, they say, to distinguish between the origins of play and its adaptive benefits. As Burghardt puts it in *The Genesis of Animal Play*, the question of why animals play "may not lie in the future-oriented practice and 'preparation for life' claims frequently made for it. The truth may lie in other directions, and be much more interesting and important."[3] In his book Burghardt explores these other directions.

After reviewing the major scholarly attempts to define play, Burghardt proposes five criteria for determining whether an activity is play. Any activity that is play will exhibit at least one characteristic from each of the criteria. These are:

1. Limited immediate function—the behavior is not fully functional in the context in which it is expressed; that is, it includes elements that do not contribute to current survival.
2. Endogenous component—the behavior is spontaneous, voluntary, pleasurable, rewarding, or autotelic ("done for its own sake").
3. Structural or temporal difference—it is different from the "serious" performance of behavior structurally or temporally, or from the way it would be carried out in "ordinary life."
4. Repeated performance—it is performed repeatedly at some point in the life span, but not rigidly or in a stereotyped manner.
5. Relaxed field—the behavior is initiated when the animal or person is adequately fed, free from stress, safe, and secure.[4]

The Evolution of Play and Sport

According to Burghardt, using these criteria allows us to recognize play or incipient play in animals that play rarely or simply as well as in behaviors that have "never previously been considered play, playlike, or precursors of play."[5] Other benefits of his five criteria are that they can account for the heterogeneity of play in terms of its origins and can link together locomotor, object, and social play.

PRIMARY, SECONDARY, AND TERTIARY PLAY

Burghardt has identified three types of play that he says "outline a broad evolutionary scenario."[6] The first of these, *primary process play*, is made possible when certain fortuitous conditions are present. These conditions include that there is excess metabolic energy and high activity levels "in a slowly developing organism with a complex behavioral repertoire" and there is protection from predation due to parental care or "some fortuitous environmental context."[7] The "relaxed field" that is made possible by being protected from predators is associated with less stimuli for the animal. In such a context animals that have excess energy and high activity levels are prone to become bored and so they seek out stimuli or create opportunities for playlike behavior. Burghardt emphasizes that primary process play itself has "no direct adaptive function at all."[8] Once such play exists it may either have no adaptive role in subsequent behavior or it may be selected to serve an evolutionary function.

Secondary and tertiary play processes are more complex forms of play that "both maintain (secondary) and enhance physiological, behavioral and mental traits in their many iterations, perhaps even fostering novel and creative behavior."[9] For example, secondary play helps to maintain physical fitness, neural processing, behavioral flexibility, and perceptual/motor coordination. And tertiary play enhances neural and behavioral development, transforms physical play to mental play, reorganizes behavior systems, and provides resources for novel behavior and creativity.[10]

According to Burghardt, the advent of parental care is particularly important for understanding the evolution of play. Generally speaking, animals, which are viable from birth (precocial) and whose behavior is governed by instinct, are the least likely to exhibit play behavior. Other animals are more helpless at birth (altricial), on the other hand, and have complex capacities that take time to develop. These animals, which need parental care for an extended period, are most likely to play. Burghardt says that with such parental care the natural selection for the maintenance of instinctual behavior was relaxed as such behavior patterns "became less necessary and even maladaptive."[11] As he puts it, "The degree of hard-wired proficiency in these behaviors decreased while other, more experientially based, supports increased." There was a "shift from closed to open genetic programmes."[12] According to Burghardt the move to experience-based learning and increased flexibility (plasticity) was important in facilitating the movement from primary process play to secondary and tertiary play processes.

Burghardt is a proponent of the "surplus resource theory" of play. As he puts it, "Play in all species,...including human beings, will be most prevalent when there are excess resources."[13] According to this theory, "species with more time and energy resources, or active in, for example, aquatic environments where costs of locomotion are reduced, would play more and this would hasten the transition between Primary, Secondary, and Tertiary play." In Burghardt's view, the question of why play is so prominent in primates is explained by this theory. He acknowledges that, given the size of their brains and complexity of their growth process, one would think that primates would spend more energy on maintenance and growth than other mammals. Recent research, however, has shown that primates, as a group, actually use less energy for maintenance and growth than other mammals.[14] If primates evolved a more efficient energetic system than other mammals, he says, "this may have hastened transitions to extensive play and resulting novel behavior and cognitive attainments."[15]

According to Burghardt, the tendency of most writers on play to confuse the fortuitous conditions that make play possible (primary process play) and play's adaptive value led to "much needless controversy" and "especially a neglect of the former in evolutionary theorizing on play."[16]

We now recognize that play can be viewed as both a product and cause of evolutionary change; that is, playful activities may be a source of enhanced behavioral and mental functioning as well as a by-product or remnant of prior evolutionary events. It is probably a mistake to think that play originally evolved in order to provide such advantages, and this mistake may have hindered a more accurate and scientifically supported analysis of play.[17]

Burghardt's research provides us with a way to understand Aquinas's insight that play is both autotelic and yet has benefits in an evolutionary context. In Burghardt's terms, play is behavior that is (1) not fully functional, (2) pleasurable and done for its own sake, (3) different from the serious behavior of ordinary life, (4) is performed repeatedly at some point in the life span, (5) takes place in a relaxed field *and also* can be related in important ways to the growth or evolution of an animal or a species.

Within Burghardt's theoretical framework, sport—as it has existed in diverse cultures throughout history—would be an example of the more complex secondary or tertiary play processes. But secondary and tertiary play depend on and build on primary process play, both as it existed in our evolutionary past and as it exists in the experiences of human beings today. Without the fortuitous conditions that provide the setting for play to emerge (both in the past and today) sport as secondary or tertiary play would not have developed.

Also, according to Burghardt, to qualify as play, secondary and tertiary play must meet at least one of the five criteria of play listed above. If we understand sport as a kind of secondary or tertiary play, the relationship between sport as enjoyable and engaged in for its own sake and the flourishing of persons is a "both/and" rather than an "either/or" phenomenon. And if one were to follow the logic of Burghardt's research, the play character of sport has a priority (ontogenetically) over its role in psychological, social, moral, or spiritual development. In this sense, the capacity of sport to be related to integral human development depends on it retaining its connection to play.

A Catholic theological approach to sport squares well with this emphasis. The experience of playing sport itself needs to be taken seriously first on its own terms, regarding its human significance. Its autonomy needs to be preserved in this sense. Only then can we begin to consider how it leads to human well-being and flourishing. Thomas Aquinas's dictum that "grace perfects nature" is the guiding principle here. Similar to the psychologists who have studied play in animals and focused on its adaptive benefits, a big part of our problem in the West—and in the United States in particular—is that we have moved too quickly to the second step of asking what play/sport is good for.

The Evolution of Play and Sport

As mentioned in chapter 2, in the early colonies and later, work was exalted and associated with godliness; play began to be viewed with a new level of suspicion and even became associated with sin. In this context it was somewhat natural, when play and sport began to be more widespread in American society, to look for their significance in relation to something else, to ask what they were good for. One answer that soon became obvious was business: sporting events could make money. But another answer was that they were good for moral or character development. In the United States today, this is still a common emphasis among Christians and many others. But if the character development approach does not first have a sound understanding of what the human significance and meaning of sport is, it doesn't get us very far. In fact, it contributes to our problems, because it ends up just being another way to instrumentalize sport, where the activity itself is at risk of being emptied of its significance. We must be careful that we don't run past the "nature" or natural part of sport, which is the only reality that God's grace can build on or "perfect."

CARDINAL RATZINGER ON SPORT

In 1978, (then) Cardinal Josef Ratzinger offered reflections on sport in an interview on the Bavarian Radio program "Zum Sonntag" (Toward Sunday), which are relevant to our discussion.[18] The interview took place just before the soccer World Cup, and Ratzinger pointed out that the global event was dominating newspaper, television, and radio coverage. Over seven hundred million people had watched the World Cup in 1970, he said, and many more would watch it in the current year. This phenomenon led Ratzinger to reflect on the appeal or drawing power of sport.

> Football has become a global event which has brought people from all around the world across all boundaries into one and the same "place for the soul," where they are united by hopes, anxieties, passions, and joy. Hardly any other event on earth can achieve a similar widespread effect. That shows that it must address something primal in people and leads us to ask where the power of sport lies.[19]

Ratzinger commented that the pessimist will point to the "bread and circuses" of ancient Rome to make their case that today we live in a decadent society that settles for trivial distractions because it knows no higher goal. But he says that this analysis does not go far enough or get to the heart of the matter. For him, the power of sport lies in the fact that it is a form of *play*. As he sees it, play fascinates us because it is associated with our desire for "fulfilled leisure" and "for a paradisiacal life."

> Because that is what play means: action, that is truly free—without a purpose and without a need to do it—while harnessing and fulfilling all of one's personal forces.
> In this sense, sport becomes a sort of foretaste of Paradise: a stepping out of the slavish earnestness of our daily life and its concerns into the free seriousness of something that should not be serious and is therefore beautiful. In that way sport overcomes daily life.[20]

Ratzinger, then, understands sport as a kind of play. It is different from ordinary life yet involves full immersion in the activity

The Evolution of Play and Sport

and is an expression of freedom. But it also has another character, "especially with children: It is a training for life." For Ratzinger, it is because sport is autotelic and yet has developmental benefits—its "both/and quality"—that makes it so intriguing. As he puts it, "It seems to me the fascination of football consists of the fact that it unites both aspects in a very persuasive manner."[21]

For Ratzinger, training for sport requires that a person "take himself in hand" and gain control over himself, in which manner he finds his way to freedom. I assume the Cardinal has in mind here the way a young athlete must be temperate in his diet, prudent in his choices, just in his relations with others, and so on. By "taking himself in hand" in this way, the young person becomes free. In team sports, the young person learns even more.

> It [sport] also teaches him...a disciplined cooperation with others. In team play, he learns to put his individuality in the service of the whole. Sport unites people in a common goal: the success and failure of each one lies in the success or failure of everyone.[22]

According to Ratzinger, the participant in sport also learns about the importance of fair play.

> And finally, sport teaches fair competition, in which the rules of the game, which everyone mutually supports, binds and unites the competitors. The freedom of playfulness, when everything is played as it should, the seriousness of competition, resolves into the freedom of a completed game.[23]

For Ratzinger, it is commercialism and money that corrupt sport and distort it in such a way that it is no longer play or an expression of freedom.

> Of course, all of this can be spoiled by commercialism, which casts the grim pall of money over everything, and changes sport into an industry which can produce an unreal world of horrifying dimensions.
>
> But this illusory world cannot exist when sport is based on positive values: as training for life and as a stepping over from our daily life in the direction of our lost Paradise.[24]

Perhaps, Ratzinger says, if we consider these dimensions of sport, "we can learn from sport to live anew."[25]

Chapter Five

THE FREEDOM OF PLAYING SPORTS

> As a free activity, play expresses some sense of what a self is; play attests to some aspect of one's "real" or "true" self. In this sense, it is a very real activity.[1]
>
> *Randolph Feezell*

IN THIS CHAPTER, I consider experiences of *playing* sport in our contemporary context in more depth with the help of the philosopher Randolph Feezell. In making the case for sport as play, Feezell draws on the work of Johan Huizinga. One of the reasons he appreciates Huizinga's work is that it takes seriously first-person *lived* experience, which correlates well with his own phenomenological method. The focus of both scholars on the lived experience of play is what makes their reflections relevant for scholars of spirituality. As a scholar of Christian spirituality, I am particularly interested in the way Feezell describes the experience of the freedom of play and play as an expression of the "true self." Freedom is a central category in Christian spirituality, after all. As St. Paul put it, "Where the Spirit of the Lord is, there is freedom" (2 Cor 3:17). For Ignatius of Loyola, the Spiritual Exercises retreat is intended to help people arrive at the interior freedom needed to recognize and respond to God's love and call in their life. And important contemporary Catholic spiritual writers often use the term *true self* as well.

SPORT AS PLAY

In an important chapter titled "A Pluralist Conception of Play," Feezell articulates a metaphysics of play. He points out that scholars have taken five approaches to play, and each tells us something important about it. These approaches are: (1) play as behavior or activity; (2) play as motive, attitude, or state of mind; (3) play as form or structure; (4) play as meaningful experience; and (5) play as an ontologically distinctive phenomenon. According to Feezell, these five approaches taken together help us to recognize the pluralism and complexity of play that must be acknowledged to understand it adequately. This thicker description of play will also help us better understand the relationship between play and sport.[2]

Play is initially categorized as a behavior, something we can see and observe throughout the animal kingdom (not only in mammals), including in human beings. Most animal species have between ten and one hundred different signals to solicit play or to ensure one another that what is about to transpire is all in good fun.[3] Play behavior can be studied from the standpoint of "understanding the paradox of behavior that is both apparently useless and yet has some adaptive advantages."[4] For human play, the concept of apparent purposelessness leads naturally to the exploration of what it means to engage in an activity for its own sake, to a consideration of the psychological dimensions of play.

Regarding play as motive, attitude, or state of mind, Feezell says that play is "an activity that requires a certain kind of attitude," that of engaging in it "as an end in itself or for intrinsic reasons."[5] He distinguishes between the pleasure of play and the pleasure of sensations associated with the sounds, tastes, smells, and sights often experienced in daily life. Drawing on the work of Fred Feldman, he distinguishes between attitudinal pleasure and such sensory pleasures. "A person takes attitudinal pleasure in some state of affairs if he enjoys it, is pleased by it, is glad that it is happening, is delighted by it."[6] For Feezell, many people experience such attitudinal pleasure in sport. He tips his hand to the next approach when he writes that he is of the view that play activities have a form or structure that distinguish them from ordinary life. This view is relevant to his discussion about whether professional athletes can be said to be playing. He disagrees with those who claim that if one is paid to play a sport, the activity can no longer be considered play. Such an approach, he thinks, overlooks the complexity of human motivations. It is possible, he claims, for an activity that has external goods associated with it to also be desired for its own sake. A professional basketball player may be happy to be paid to play the game he has loved since childhood, for example. And he would still play it even if he were not being paid to do so.

As mentioned, for Feezell play activities have a particular form or structure that sets them apart from ordinary life. Some authors write about play activities as on a continuum from the least to most formal. Play can be splashing water in a bathtub, frolicking on the beach, or a game that has rules and requires skills. Play doesn't need to be formal as it is in games, but it often is in human societies. As was mentioned in chapter 1, we can think of games as having "prelusory goals," such as putting a golf ball into a cup. But in the game of golf, the ways one can put the ball in the cup are proscribed by the constitutive rules of the game. The most efficient ways of doing so, such as walking up to the cup and dropping the ball in, are ruled out. Not only that, but the game introduces gratuitous challenges. Putting the ball into the cup with these and other challenges added is the "lusory goal" of the game. Bernard Suits summarizes what it means to play a game with these formal or structural elements:

> To play a game is to attempt to achieve a specific state of affairs..., using only means permitted by rules..., where the rules prohibit use of more efficient in favor of less efficient means..., and where such rules are accepted just because they make possible such activity.[7]

Playing games that have intrinsic rewards and are structured in a way that makes them different from ordinary life is also a meaningful experience. According to Feezell, some of the ways people describe the meaningfulness of play are that it is an experience of freedom, intrinsic meaning, purposelessness, inherent attraction, spontaneity, diminished consciousness of self, unselfing, absorption, responsive openness, attunement, union, and fun.[8]

For Hans Georg Gadamer, play is also an ontologically distinctive phenomenon. When at play we are drawn out of ourselves into the larger world of "the game," with its own demands, structure, and intrinsic meaning that absorb "the player into itself." Gadamer's understanding helps to ground the oft-expressed view today that "the game" is bigger than those of us who play it and, therefore, must be respected in its own right. Indeed, for Gadamer, when the game is played, the "real subject of the game...is not the player, but instead the game itself." But this doesn't mean that play has no intrinsic or subjective meaning for the player. On the contrary, the very emphasis on the game as the subject of play helps us to understand this meaningfulness. "What holds the player in its spell, draws him into play, and keeps him there is the game itself." And because the game is played for its own sake, "play is really limited to presenting itself. Thus its mode of being is self-presentation."[9]

At the end of this chapter, Feezell returns to the question of whether sport is a kind of play. He says there are two main objections to this position, both having to do with sport being infected by desires that are incompatible with play. The first one has already been mentioned: The view that professional athletes cannot be said to be playing because they are being paid. According to this view, such persons have instrumental rather than autotelic motivation. Such an approach, Feezell claims, reduces play to attitudinal considerations and "[ignores] the relevance of other properties [of sport], structural and experiential." For him, the form or structure of sport as an activity has "play-like properties," as we have seen. This objection also rules out the possibility that a player can enjoy playing his sport and appreciate its intrinsic rewards *and also* be happy that he is being paid to play. For Feezell, even if the adherents of this position are right about the relationship between play and professional sport, in most other contexts in which sport is practiced, it has properties associated with play, such as "freedom, separateness, absorption, purposelessness."[10]

The second objection has to do with the role of the desire to win in sport. From this perspective, sport is incompatible with play because of its competitive nature. For adherents of this view, competition is rule-governed and associated with extrinsic motivations (for social approval, for example); it is product rather than process oriented. In competitive sport, the person is no longer engaged in an activity for its own sake, but for the goal of winning. Feezell is sympathetic to this view's emphasis on the dangers of competition, but he thinks it is important to resist the notion that play cannot be competitive or rule-governed. This seems to reduce play to frolic. A better approach would be to acknowledge that there are "more or less formal modes of play." Rules are created for noncompetitive games such as leapfrog and for competitive games that have an internal goal (winning). "Certainly playing a game, attempting to overcome unnecessary obstacles, or freely confronting gratuitous difficulty, may be engaged in for the sake of the activity, even if the activity has an internal end that cannot be shared by the victor and the vanquished."[11] Such activities may or may not also have extrinsic goods associated with them (social status, money, fame), but these must be considered along with other factors when we are determining whether an activity is play or not.

Feezell concludes his chapter with reflections on the way some important contemporary writers on play "attempt to rouse us out of the doldrums of ordinary existence by awakening (or reawakening) in us moments of joy, exuberance, creativity, spontaneity, freedom, optimism, and fun," which we associate with our younger days but often lose touch with along the way. And in this sense, these authors are connecting play to "a notion of a good human life" and are of the view that "sport should be placed in the context of play and living well—joyously, freely, creatively."[12] Feezell closes with these words:

> Given what we have said about the variety of approaches to play, the fecundity of play phenomena, and the connection between play and a good human life, we should reinforce, whenever it is appropriate, the notion that sport is found in the neighborhood

of play. In addition, we should do this in order to encourage the enchanting possibilities of sport, play, and life itself. When we find that sport has strayed from its natural home, we must encourage the wayward child to come back from the world.[13]

WHAT IS FREEDOM?

Feezell follows Huizinga in understanding play as a free activity. But what does it mean to say that an activity is free? Many authors emphasize the connection between freedom and choice. For Feezell, however, it is not necessary that play *start* by the free choice of the individual. For example, a young girl can be sent outside to play by her mother when she wanted to stay inside and watch television. And anyone who has played on a team knows that one doesn't always feel like practicing or even playing a game when it is time to do so. For Feezell, what is most important is what the person is experiencing *while engaged in the activity*. Once a person is engaged in an activity, if that person "affirms, embraces, or identifies" with it and experiences enjoyment while doing so, then he or she is experiencing the freedom of play. During such experiences, because the person identifies with what he or she is doing, the person is also expressing him- or herself.

This makes sense in light of my own experiences as a young person playing on teams. On many occasions I didn't want to go to practice, because it was held too early in the morning, or I was tired, or I was with my girlfriend. But when I arrived at practice, often I became fully immersed in what we were doing, identified with it, and enjoyed it. The activity became a context for me to express something of myself. At such times, it did seem like I was experiencing the freedom of play.[14]

Feezell's understanding of the freedom of play is influenced by the philosopher Frithjof Bergmann. For Bergmann, freedom is not only a matter of being able to choose among options *a*, *b*, and *c*, and so on. Indeed, it is possible to have many options and even choose one of them without being free. I may have chosen an option out of an exaggerated need for security, because I'm afraid of what others will think, or because I think it will bring me wealth or fame. Over time I may discover, as I live out an option, that it grinds against something in me. I might feel "this is not who I am." In Bergmann's view, this would be an experience of unfreedom.

For Bergmann, neither does freedom require the removal of all causes or external influences. "We do not think that it signifies anything like independence from all influence, or 'autonomy'—when that idea isolates the individual from the world."[15] A decision can be influenced by external factors, events outside of one's control, or other people and still be free. And certainly, some causes or influences help us make good decisions. These include an education that broadens our perspective, the wise counsel of a friend or elder, or a supportive community.

One can even have significant constraints or hindrances in life and still be free in important respects. Bergmann's view on this matter is influenced by the fact that he grew up in Nazi Germany with a Jewish mother. Even in this context, he writes that

> life was not bereft of choices. There always were conversations, on trains and in buses, to which one could either listen in silence, or in which one could ask a variety of risky questions. Even in the notorious salute, one could either lift one's hand as if one

was very tired, or raise one's arm so that it snapped like a triggered wooden board. The constant hum of choices never stopped, and they were anything but insignificant.[16]

An exaggeration of the "magnitude of the political,"[17] he writes, prevents us from understanding that "governments cannot give or take away the dignity of man, any more than they can do this with his freedom."[18]

For Bergmann, it is more accurate to understand freedom in relation to identity. As he puts it, "The primary condition of freedom is the possession of an identity, or of a self—freedom is the acting out of that identity."[19] According to Bergmann, the experience of freedom occurs when the self identifies with the deliberations that give rise to some proposed action in the world and the ensuing activity. He uses the writings of Plato, Aristotle, and Dostoevsky to illustrate that prominent philosophers and writers have understood freedom in this way. These thinkers each have a different understanding of what constitutes a human being. But they share the view that when a person acts from his authentic humanity and identifies with the deliberations that give rise to an action and the ensuing activity, that person is experiencing freedom. Because the person identifies with the deliberations and what he is doing, he is also expressing himself.

When it comes to making sense of our everyday life in the world, Bergmann's emphasis on identity replaces the usual associations of freedom with having options or autonomy with the idea of correspondence. From this perspective, when we are making decisions about our life it is helpful to think of freedom in terms of a "matching" between who we are and what we are doing.

PLAY, SPORT, AND SPIRIT

> Our outward life has to match our identity or our self if we are to attain freedom. We have to achieve something like a geometrical congruence, a mutual fit, a kind of attunedness, like a harmony between two tones. There should therefore be a basic sense of ease, as when two gears spin without friction in a prearranged synchronization. The usual stress on the difficulty of freedom...should begin to have some slight ring of melodrama and of pathos, and just the reverse side should make itself felt: the absence of strain, the collapse of tension, the lightness of freedom, glorious as that of pure play.[20]

For Bergmann, because of the congruence between our identity and our outward life, freedom in this sense will have a natural and "spontaneous flow"[21] to it. It won't feel cramped or forced, and there will be a shift away from the need to control, compensate, and correct, "toward the exuberance of actions and words at last taking shape quite effortlessly, as if by themselves."[22] And we work backward from these kinds of felt experiences to understanding who we are.

> We discover ourselves only indirectly, and often from the "feel" of certain actions. It is this increase in vitality and surefootedness, this undertaking of a shift that ends with the definite impression of one's now "having found one's stride," of one's now "functioning" that is by all accounts one of the surest indications that an accord with our nature has been found.[23]

On the other hand, for Bergmann, when the self is dissociated from the deliberations giving rise to action and the ensuing activity, the person is unfree. And the felt experience of unfreedom is the opposite of that of freedom. As he puts it,

> If freedom could be symbolized as a correspondence, as a harmony, and if the free man [*sic*] basically expresses what he really is, then unfreedom is a conflict, a dissonance. The outward life and conduct of the unfree man are unattuned and grate against his inner nature.[24]

According to Bergmann, there is also a moral dimension to consider when discussing freedom. It is important that a person be self-aware enough to acknowledge that not all his impulses or character traits are good or to be encouraged. "It is not true or legitimate," he writes, "to say simply, 'The more freedom the better.'"[25]

> I know that some parts of me are pretty vile and that expressing those will make me worse. And the same goes for others: they, too, have some foul qualities and it is natural that these should be restrained.... If some people can express their identifications only through the manipulation of great economic power, then we might point out to them that not every expression of the self is sacred.[26]

THE FREEDOM OF PLAY

Bergmann's way of understanding freedom helps us to understand what we mean when we say that play is a free activity. As mentioned earlier, for Feezell a person doesn't have to freely choose to begin an activity for it to be play. What is most important is what he is experiencing while engaged in the activity.

> Whether the player voluntarily begins to play—and, admittedly, he usually does—the important feature of the activity is that while it is being undertaken, the player identifies with what he is doing. At the heart of play is a strong sense of affirmation on the part of the player, and this affirmative "yea-saying" spirit is an essential part of the player's stance. This also accounts for the sense in which play is often deeply enjoyable or pleasurable.[27]

Bergmann's emphasis on the importance of having a self or identity for being able to experience freedom also helps us to understand why when young children specialize in one sport too early this often leads to problems such as burnout and dropping out.[28] The most basic issue is that it takes time to develop a sense of identity, and young children haven't had the time to do so yet. This means that they cannot identify with what they are doing in Bergmann's sense and engage in "yea-saying," which is also self-expression. In other words, they can't experience the freedom of play.

Rather, the dynamic that often unfolds is that they try to *earn* a sense of self or identity through a successful outcome. According to Jay Coakley, "This means that every mistake, every loss, and every time that perfection is not reached spins these athletes into emotional turmoil and creates doubt about their competence…and their self-worth as a person." For Coakley, it is better to give young people the space and time to grow up and develop a sense of their identity and then let them make choices about whether to play sports or decide which sports to play. In this way, they will feel more of a sense of "ownership" in relation to their sport.[29] In Bergmann's terms, when they have a self that is able to identify with—"yea-say"—their sport and their engagement in it, they will be able to experience the freedom of play.

The identification with what he is doing and the "yea-saying" also mean that the person who is experiencing the freedom of play in sport is engaged in what Gadamer calls "self-presentation." According to Gadamer, when one spends oneself in a game "one is in fact playing oneself out. The self-presentation of the game involves the player's achieving, as it were, his own self-presentation by playing—i.e., presenting—something."[30] We have likely witnessed this phenomenon when watching our favorite athletes play. For my generation, Los Angeles Laker Magic Johnson epitomized this "playing oneself out" with his contagious smile accompanying his exuberant play and creativity on the court. Perhaps many of us have also experienced this kind of self-presentation while at play ourselves, albeit in less public ways.

This helps us to understand what it means—and does not mean—to say that play is separate from ordinary or "real life." It doesn't mean that it is "unreal." As Feezell puts it, "As a free activity, play expresses some sense of what a self is; play attests to some aspect of one's 'real' or 'true' self. In this sense it is a very real activity." It is true that in structured and formally organized sports, a "play world is constituted by rules and boundaries of space and time," which separates and distinguishes the activity from the rest of ordinary life. This is why sport as play is sometimes described as "unreal, make-believe, and separate. But as a form of play, participation in sports is still a free activity that expresses something with which a self identifies."[31]

According to Feezell, this way of understanding the freedom of play is enlightening. It has been common in the United

States to think of play as the opposite of work. In this context, play is usually considered something frivolous that children engage in or as a distraction from work. "The work ethic is proclaimed as the sacred ethic of life," he writes.[32] But he suggests that instead of thinking of play only in relation to childish irresponsibility or as a distraction from what is really important, we should think of it as a natural outflow of the self.

> That is, think of play as an activity expressive of some real part of a self and it becomes apparent that people should play more, not less. Those times when we *feel* most free, less tense or strained, and most lighthearted are times in which we are involved in something like a playful activity. We should also like our vocation to be something that tangentially approaches the play experience, for our vocation would then be in liberating coincidence with our true selves.[33]

THE FREEDOM OF PLAY AND EMBODIMENT

The tendency in the modern world and especially in U.S. culture to understand play in opposition to work is part of the reason scholars have not taken play and sport seriously until recently. But another reason for the lack of attention is because of a body-mind dualism that has been a characteristic of modernity and is still present in new forms in our context. René Descartes played an important role in this regard in the seventeenth century when he introduced a new dualism of body and soul (which he equated with mind). He described body and soul in terms of their formal properties, with the body being material, extended in space and unconscious, and the soul being immaterial, unextended in space and conscious. This formulation made it very difficult for philosophers who came after him to understand how the embodied experiences of human beings affected consciousness and our thinking. In this context, the lived experience of the body became less important to pay attention to. After all, identity and freedom were associated with the mind, as captured in Descartes's famous saying, "I think, therefore I am."[34]

But if freedom has to do with self-expression, as Bergmann claims, it is also necessarily a bodily phenomenon. How else can we express ourselves as human beings except in and through our bodies? As Maurice Merleau-Ponty put it, "My body is the seat or rather the very actuality of the phenomenon of expression."[35] And sport is a very rich context within which such embodied self-expression can occur. According to Klaus Meier,

> Play, and in particular playful sport, as a vibrant form of human endeavor, reveals the body in its lived concreteness. Configurations and meanings inscribed with shapes and qualities expressive and indicative of the texture of the being of the participant arise by means of the body's power of expression.[36]

Merleau-Ponty's conviction that consciousness is always embodied also means that when playing a sport, a person will be able to arrive at new insights into himself and his relationships with others, and even into the meaning of his life. As Meier puts it,

> It is through the power and gestures of the "lived-body," fully and openly engaged in dialogue with the world, that [the person] discloses, establishes, and

broadens the personal meanings of his existence. Moments of "intense realness" available in sport provide opportunities for the unfolding of new insights and the restructuring of previous perceptions.[37]

From a contemporary theological perspective, the importance of embodiment for the experience of freedom makes sense as well. Margaret Farley points out that it has been common for theologians, even in the recent past, to think of freedom "as a capacity of the spirit,...with the body being simply the object or instrument of our choice in some way." However, as she puts it,

> our bodies are not purely passive, not appendages, not merely instruments for our selves; they are intrinsic to our selves....Our motivations for choice, actions of choice, and choice itself are embodied and inspirited. Hence, it is as embodied spirits, inspirited bodies, that we are self-transcendent through our freedom.[38]

For Pope Benedict XVI, experiences of the freedom of play in sports can help people to understand and appreciate the meaning of their embodiment. In a speech to Italian ski instructors, he said that participation in sports teaches "the harmonization of important dimensions of the human being, favouring their integral development. Through sports, a person understands better that his body cannot be considered an object; rather, through corporeity, he expresses himself and enters into relations with others."[39]

The Freedom of Playing Sports

FREEDOM AND CHRISTIAN SPIRITUALITY

Bergmann recognizes that his way of understanding freedom correlates well with the way it is understood in religious and spiritual traditions. In these traditions, autonomy is not held up as the highest value. Rather, what is most important is the willingness to be led and guided by God (Yahweh, Allah, Tao, etc.) and a person's being in right relationship with others and all created reality.

> In some cultures and religions, surrender and acceptance open up the door to wisdom, and...this attitude may be spread far more widely than its opposite, which may even be peculiarly "Western."...The surrender of the insistence on the privilege of one's own choice can be seen as a step bringing one closer to what is really home, and not only as the moment in which one's [humanity] is cut off.[40]

Bergmann's understanding of freedom correlates well with what Christian spiritual writers call "interior freedom," with respect to both its structure and its content. Identification is logically prior to interior freedom; such freedom is not a primary but a derivative notion. The Christian believes that God created the world and everything in it freely and out of love. The human person is created in love and for love. This is the human person's identity. God is also laboring in the world, continuing to bring all of creation to redemption and fullness of life. The dynamic of the Spiritual Exercises retreat of Ignatius of Loyola is meant to help a person to have a felt experience of being loved by God (identity) and arrive at interior freedom from attachments so he or she can respond to God's love, say "Yes." What makes the kind of identification Ignatius describes distinctive is that it is identification with what God is doing in the world, who is the source from which *everything* flows.[41]

Spiritual Consolation

According to Ignatius, for the person who is "progressing from good to better"[42] in the Christian life, it is important to pay attention to one sort of affective experience that he called *spiritual consolation*. It is helpful when trying to understand what Ignatius means by spiritual consolation to begin with what the term consolation ordinarily means, that is, affective experiences such as inner peace, gladness, sweetness, well-being.[43] For Ignatius, the person in spiritual consolation experiences such feelings as peace, tears, genuine happiness, and spiritual joy.[44] What makes consolation *spiritual* is that the person experiences God's loving and guiding hand in the peace, sweetness, tears, joy, or delight and is explicitly encouraged in his faith and trust in God. He has a felt experience of an "increase in hope, faith and charity."[45] He is also strengthened during these times and often has new ideas and inspirations.

Ignatius's guidelines for discernment have some analogies to Feezell's description of the freedom of play. The images Ignatius uses suggests there is an ease and effortlessness to the experience of God's action in the life of a person who is progressing from good to better, for example. As he puts it, God (sometimes through the mediation of his "good spirit" or "good angels") "makes things easier and eliminates all obstacles, so that the persons may move forward in doing good."[46] When describing the experiences of consolation for persons who are further along in the Christian life, he says that God "touches the soul gently, lightly, and sweetly, like a drop of water going into a sponge." Because the person is already going from good to better, it feels like the "good spirit" is entering "silently, like those who go into their own house by an open door."[47]

Ignatius expected persons would experience spiritual consolation in their everyday life. And like Bergmann, he thought that we work backward from these kinds of experiences to understand who we are and what our vocation is. This is why the Examen prayer is recommended, which involves in our contemporary understanding reflecting on our day and taking note of experiences of spiritual consolation (as well as spiritual desolation, about which more later). At times in our daily life, we notice there is a matching or a syncing up between who we are and what we are doing. According to Dean Brackley, SJ, it is important to pay attention to these experiences to discover our vocation. As he puts it, during such experiences "something 'clicks.' We have found what we were born for."[48]

What makes the experience of spiritual consolation distinctive in relation to Bergmann's notion of identification is the theological dimension. From a theological perspective, the reason the person experiences congruence and effortlessness is that the Holy Spirit is leading the person in the same basic direction that the person is already going in. The Holy Spirit and the "spirit" of the person are in sync. There is a "matching" in this sense.[49] William Barry, SJ, describes this kind of experience as being "attuned to the one action of God, to his will." According to Barry, this attunement or matching occurs simultaneously with a matching between a person's identity and what they are doing.

> In such a state you are a contemplative in action. You know that you are at the right place at the right time. There are no doubts about whether you should be someone else or somewhere else. You do not need

> to justify being married or single or a religious;...
> it is right to be who you are here and now. And you
> live and act comfortably with the knowledge of your
> own limitations, of your finitude, of your small part
> in the immense history of the world.[50]

For Barry, this is an experience of freedom, happiness, and fulfillment that can be had even amidst sorrow and pain in the world.

> To be attuned to the one action of God, to his will, is
> to be extraordinarily free, happy, and fulfilled even
> in the midst of a world of sorrow and pain. One can,
> perhaps, understand how Jesus could celebrate the
> Last Supper even though he knew in his bones it
> would be [his] "last."[51]

Spiritual Desolation

For Ignatius, persons who are trying to go from good to better in the Christian life will also experience *spiritual desolation*. And the felt experience of spiritual desolation is the opposite of spiritual consolation. While spiritual desolation is experienced throughout one's life, it is common for persons to struggle with it early in their commitment to living the Christian life, or when they are considering or beginning a new work or ministry. This is why Ignatius spends more time on spiritual desolation than consolation in his earliest guidelines for discernment. As with spiritual consolation, it helps to understand spiritual desolation to start with what the term *desolation* means in ordinary speech. As a state of consciousness, the term ordinarily refers to affective states such as distress, gloom, discouragement, and loss of hope.[52] According to Ignatius,

The Freedom of Playing Sports

when in spiritual desolation the person experiences dryness or tepidity in relation to God and spiritual things, a wandering of attention to momentary pleasures, confusion, and disquiet from various agitations and temptations.[53] Indeed, the experience of spiritual desolation is *spiritual* because the dryness, confusion, and sadness are experienced explicitly as tempting the person to trust God less, to slacken their prayer practices, and so on. If these temptations are not handled well, spiritual desolation can weaken a person's faith, hope, and love.

For Ignatius, whereas God's presence and activity in a person going from good to better is associated with a sense of ease and effortlessness, the one he calls the "enemy of our human nature" causes anxiety and sets up obstacles to prevent the person's progress. For those who are further along in the Christian life, it is characteristic of "the enemy," he says, to cause disquiet and to fight against genuine happiness and spiritual consolation. In such cases, the enemy touches the soul "sharply, with noise and disturbance, like a drop of water falling onto a stone."[54]

When we are in the process of making a significant life decision, spiritual desolation may be a sign that we are moving in the wrong direction. Consider one example: Soon after Michael had made the Spiritual Exercises retreat over the course of nine months, he was offered a new job as a researcher at a major state university in the area of basic radiological sciences. He had for some time been feeling dissatisfied with the company he had been working at, which had many problems and even some core values that conflicted with his own. When he told his former employer about the new job offer, his employer offered him more money and new responsibilities. When he engaged in an imaginative exercise where he pictured himself staying with his former company, he noticed he felt disturbed and agitated. "There was just such an agitation with staying where I was....It was an agitation, but it wasn't a neutral thing. It just definitely seemed to me to be more about an enticement and a lure that I could rationalize taking, because maybe I was called to be in this place and help straighten things out or whatever. The appeals were all to my ego."[55]

> And I call that a discernment because there were so many things enticing me to stay in the familiar environment with the people I had come to know and stay where I was living and just change titles and salary and grow into that spot. There were things that on the surface looked very right about that. Very right. But the process for me was that I just had to keep listening to what was underneath all of that. What were the movements that I was experiencing under that? In which of these two decisions did I feel more at peace? and have more hope? and have a sense that this was going to flow out into something very fruitful in the world?[56]

When imagining himself staying with his old company, Michael felt agitation rather than peace and didn't feel hopeful. On the other hand, when he imagined himself taking the new position at the university, he said, "Something was very correct, very right about it. That was very present, this rightness, this sort of lightness, I'll say. Just very correct....This sense of connecting with the people, what the job was, a lightness about it, a sense of hopefulness about it—all this just said, 'This is it!'"[57]

The reader will notice that Ignatius's description of spiritual desolation (and Michael's experience of it) has some analogies with Bergmann's description of unfreedom. For Bergmann, the person experiences unfreedom as a "conflict, a dissonance."[58] He feels there is an "unattunement" in such cases between who he is and his outward life. What he is doing grates against his "inner nature" or true self.⁵⁹ He experiences this as a loss of harmony, vitality, and flow in his life.

Michael's experiences of agitation when he imagined himself staying with his former employer and taking the additional money and responsibilities were an indication to him that he would not be living out of his true self if he had stayed with his former company, even though "on the surface" a lot "looked very right" about doing so. His process led him to listen to what was "underneath all of that." When he imagined himself taking the new job, he experienced freedom in Bergmann's sense: a matching between his identity and what he would be doing, which felt "very right, very correct," "connecting with the people, what the job was," and left him feeling a lightness and hopefulness, a sense that this work would "flow out into something...fruitful."

Given everything I have written so far, it may not be surprising to learn that Ignatius counsels that our major decisions in life should be made related to and building on experiences of spiritual consolation. As he put it in a letter to Teresa Rejadell, genuine spiritual consolation "points out and opens up for us the path we should follow and the contrary path we should avoid."⁶⁰ It does us well, then, to pay attention to our experiences of spiritual consolation and to notice what we are drawn to at those times. Ignatius gives this advice in his Spiritual Exercises for times when the retreatant is experiencing both spiritual consolation and desolation. When the retreatant is not experiencing such movements of spirit, Ignatius provides other ways to help a person make a decision, involving the use of one's reason or imagination.⁶¹

True Self

Now I will explore the way contemporary Christian spiritual writers understand the term *true self* in dialogue with Feezell. Some Christian writers use *true self* to refer to the self that is

PLAY, SPORT, AND SPIRIT

created in the image and likeness of God. As Thomas Merton puts it, "Our true self is the person we are meant to be—...free and upright, in the image and likeness of God."[62] According to Merton, the Church Fathers understood sin as having the effect of defacing or diminishing the image and likeness of God in ourselves and others (who are affected by sin). And they understood the process of redemption to be a matter of recovering the true self, underneath layers of unlikeness and distortions. "Thus we are repairing the image of God in us," as Bernard of Clairvaux put it.[63] In this sense, we are all in "recovery."

For Merton, the human being is different from plants, trees, and other animals. God makes each individual plant, tree, or animal what it is, and it gives glory to God by simply existing in this way.

> The special clumsy beauty of this particular colt on this April day in this field under these clouds is a holiness consecrated to God by his own creative wisdom and it declares the glory of God.[64]

With us it is different, however. It is not enough to "be what our nature intends."[65] We are free to be ourselves or not.

> God leaves us free to be whatever we like. We can be ourselves or not, as we please. We are at liberty to be real, or to be unreal. We may be true or false, the choice is ours. We may wear now one mask and now another, and never, if we so desire, appear with our own true face.[66]

For Merton, by collaborating with what God is doing in our lives and in the world, we play a role in creating our own identity. As he puts it,

Our vocation is not simply to *be*, but to work together with God in the creation of our own life, our own identity, our own destiny. We are free beings and sons [and daughters] of God. This means to say that we should not passively exist, but actively participate in His creative freedom, in our own lives, and in the lives of others, by choosing the truth. To put it better, we are even called to share with God the work of *creating* the truth of our identity.[67]

"Actively participat[ing] in God's creative freedom" is an instance of the "identification" Bergmann writes about in the broadest possible context. And there are "two freedoms" involved in this process, as Merton points out.[68] Fr. Matthew, from Merton's monastic community, described the dynamic of participating in God's creative freedom as a kind of dancing.

We have but to live, take each day as it comes,… and have a kind of response to the will of God that is much like dancing. You must work with it. It is not a matter of passive submission. This [is] no way to dance; it is too heavy, too leaden, too dragging and uninspired. No, you must dance with your partner, you must cooperate, you must work with the will of God. This is the sort of dancing that leads to the kingdom and makes one free.[69]

For Merton, when the dance is going well, we appear "with our own true face." And this is what sanctity is. "For me to be a saint means to be myself," he writes. "Therefore the problem of sanctity and salvation is in fact the problem of finding out who I am and of discovering my true self."[70]

PLAY, SPORT, AND SPIRIT

Themes in the poetry of Jesuit poet Gerard Manley Hopkins also have resonances with Feezell's writings about the true self. Hopkins sees all of creation to be engaged in a sort of self-expression, which he describes in his poem "As Kingfishers Catch Fire":

> As kingfishers catch fire, dragonflies dráw fláme;
> As tumbled over rim in roundy wells
> Stones ring; like each tucked string tells, each hung bell's
> Bow swung finds tongue to fling out broad its name;
> Each mortal thing does one thing and the same;
> Deals out that being indoors each one dwells;
> Selves—goes itself; *myself* it speaks and spells;
> Crying *Whát I dó is me: for that I came.*[71]

For Feezell and Hopkins, when a human being lives in such a way there is a "matching" between who he is and his outward actions is a sign that he is living out his vocation. When Hopkins writes, "What I do is me," he doesn't mean "I am what I produce." Rather, he means that what I am doing is an expression of who I am. He continues:

> Í say móre: the just man justices;
> Kéeps grace: thát keeps all his goings graces;
> Acts in God's eye what in God's eye he is—
> Chríst—for Christ plays in ten thousand places,
> Lovely in limbs, and lovely in eyes not his
> To the Father through the features of men's faces.[72]

It is significant that Hopkins describes this dynamic of persons being their true selves as Christ *playing* in "ten thousand places." For Hopkins, when we become as Christ is—beloved sons and daughters of the Father living in freedom—our lives take on a playlike quality and it is "lovely" to behold.

The Freedom of Play and Vocation

Indeed, according to Merton, when we have a felt sense of our identity as a beloved son or daughter of God and are "yea-saying" what God is doing in the world, our vocation can be experienced as a kind of play. He expresses this in a letter to Jacques Maritain, in which he encouraged the philosopher to realize he is entirely in God's love and care and not to worry about anything.

> Do not push too hard with the work, God will take care of everything, and will give you strength to do all that needs to be done. The rest is in His hands. Realize yourself to be entirely in His love and His care and worry about nothing. In these days you should be carried by Him toward your destination, and do what you do more as play than as work, which does not mean that it is not serious: for the most serious thing in the life of a Christian is play.[73]

For Merton, play is not trivial or a distraction that gets in the way of our work, but is the very mode of being that is associated with fruitful labor. This makes sense from a psychological perspective. When we enjoy our work and it is intrinsically rewarding (two key indicators of play), we gladly go beyond minimum requirements. In the process we will likely introduce something new and push the boundaries of our field. This has relevance for all kinds of work. Walter Ong, SJ, in his preface to Hugo Rahner's book *Man at Play*, writes,

PLAY, SPORT, AND SPIRIT

> The best workers in any field are those for whom their work is a kind of play—the mechanic whose job serves his desire to "tinker" with machines, the basic research engineer who is "playing around" with various possibilities for a huge industrial complex, the financier who "plays the market," the philosopher who likes to "play" with ideas.[74]

Ong's understanding of how work can be experienced as a kind of play correlates well with Feezell's understanding of the freedom of play as self-expression. For Ong, this happens when one's work is "free in the sense that it truly comes from within, comes as a realization of human potential, as an effusion of activity spilling out from an immanent source. Work is an expression of freedom and joy. But this is what play itself is."[75]

For Ong, the writings of Johan Huizinga and others on play are highly pertinent for Christian theology, "which is concerned with a God who is good and thus 'diffusive of himself,' spontaneously and freely giving first existence and then redemption to his creatures, who are thus the result of his play."[76] He praises Hugo Rahner for writing about play and so explicating

> in a fresh way the freedom of the children of God, which is a participation in the freedom of God himself. God's activity toward and in all his creation is like that germinal, undifferentiated activity of the child, which is both work and play, both serious application and spontaneous activity for its own sake. Thus only those who "become as little children" can enter the kingdom of heaven.[77]

The Freedom of Playing Sports

According to Ong, it is common in our experience in U.S. culture for work and play to drift apart after childhood, although they never lose contact entirely. "With God," he writes, "such separation never comes. God's work is always play in the sense that it is always joyous, spontaneous, and completely free."[78] This is why when the Christian identifies with what "God the player" is doing in the world he is also able to experience the freedom of play and express his true self.

Chapter Six

THE JOY OF PLAYING SPORTS

> Man at play, as thinkers from Plato to Sartre have observed, is at the peak of his freedom and dignity....Perhaps Plato was right, and it is possible after all to "live life as play." But in [the] last quarter of the twentieth century... the intuitive grasp of playfulness is difficult to recapture.[1]
>
> *Mihaly Csikszentmihalyi*

I MENTIONED IN THE FIRST CHAPTER that when Johan Huizinga was writing *Homo Ludens: The Study of the Play Element in Culture*, he raised concerns that scholars had not studied play itself, but instead focused on the ways it functioned as a means to other ends. He pointed out that physiologists and psychologists "all start from the assumption that play must serve something which is *not* play" but "most of them only deal incidentally with the question of what play is *in itself* and what it means for the player."[2] Gordon Burghardt expressed a similar concern regarding scientists who focus on animal play only as a means to evolutionary benefits or advantages.

The psychologist Mihaly Csikszentmihalyi expressed similar concerns at the beginning of his academic career in the 1970s. He pointed out that ethological psychologists emphasized how play is a way for young organisms to learn in relatively safe environments so that they don't have to pay too high a price for errors. Others, like Erik Erikson and Jean Piaget, highlighted the way play strengthened the ego or aided the development of an autonomous moral self. "These approaches leave out one of the main aspects of play," Csikszentmihalyi wrote, "which is the simple fact that it is enjoyable in itself. Regardless of whether it decreases anxiety or increases competence, play is fun. The question of why play is enjoyable has rarely been asked directly."[3]

Csikszentmihalyi made such an important contribution to the field of psychology early in his career precisely because he addressed this question. He became interested in understanding enjoyment in play and other activities while doing his doctoral research about the dynamics of the creative process in artists. At the time, he was studying artists who had been painting for many years, and yet had little expectation that their paintings would bring them much in the way of external rewards, such as wealth or fame. These artists truly enjoyed what they were doing. He was intrigued by the fact that they would completely immerse themselves in the painting process and derived satisfaction from discussing the subtleties of their craft, "small technical details, stylistic breakthroughs, the actions, thoughts, and feelings involved in making art. Slowly it became obvious, that something in the activity of painting itself kept them going."[4]

Csikszentmihalyi pointed out that the most influential psychological schools, such as depth psychology or behaviorism, were not able to adequately account for what he was observing. A depth psychologist would have focused on the way the painters' motivation had to do with resolving psychosexual conflicts from childhood, and a behavioral psychologist would have tried to understand how external rewards motivated their behavior. Neither would have been interested in understanding the enjoyment of painting itself. This is what Csikszentmihalyi wanted to understand.

AUTOTELIC ACTIVITIES AND ENJOYMENT

To better understand enjoyment in play and other activities, Csikszentmihalyi and his researchers studied people engaged in autotelic activities. As mentioned earlier, the word *autotelic* comes from Greek words, *auto* = self and *telos* = goal, indicating that an activity has its goal or purpose within itself. Regarding motivation, people participate in such activities for their own sake. One famous music composer expressed this autotelic mentality well:

> One doesn't do it for money....This is what I tell my students. Don't expect to make money, don't expect fame or a pat on the back, don't expect a damn thing. Do it because you love it.[5]

Csikszentmihalyi's early contribution to the field of psychology came about in large part because of his attention to play. His own research had been influenced by the scholarly literature on play, but one of the limitations of such literature, in his estimation, was the way it tended to understand play as separate from ordinary or real life. This approach assumed an unbridgeable gap between the way people experience play and work.

He questioned whether such a gap existed. And so to address this issue he studied enjoyment as people experience it both at play (rock climbers, chess players, female dancers, and basketball players) and at work (music composers, teachers, and surgeons). All work has an external goal (it is "exotelic"), but he discovered that sometimes composers, teachers, and surgeons described what they were doing as enjoyable and having intrinsic meaning and rewards as well.[6] The composer quoted above is a good example of this phenomenon. Csikszentmihalyi comments,

> All the evidence from our investigations suggests that the essential difference is not between "play" and "work"…but between the "flow" experience (which typically occurs in play activities but may be present in work as well) and the experience of anxiety or boredom (which may occur at any time and any place but is more likely in activities that provide either too few or too many opportunities for action).[7]

While people often experience flow in play activities, flow and play are not synonymous. Flow can be experienced in other activities as well. According to Csikszentmihalyi, "almost any description of the creative experience…includes experiential accounts that are in important respects analogous" to flow.[8] He also wrote that

> besides play and creativity, experiences analogous to flow have been reported in contexts usually called "transcendental" or "religious." Maslow's peak experiences and De Charm's "origin" state share many

distinctive features with the flow process. The same is true of accounts of collective ritual; of the practice of Zen, Yoga, and other forms of meditation; or of practically any other form of religious experience.[9]

In the last part of this chapter, I will consider some analogies between experiences of flow and the dynamics of the Christian life and vocation.[10]

PLEASURE OR ENJOYMENT?

Based on the way people described their experiences, Csikszentmihalyi made a distinction between pleasure and enjoyment. Most people, he writes, when thinking of the kinds of experiences that improve the quality of life, first think of pleasurable experiences associated with "good food, good sex, all the comforts money can buy."[11] He points out that such experiences can improve the quality of life, but on their own they do not lead to happiness. For one thing, pleasurable experiences don't require much attention or investment on the part of the person and hence don't lead to their growth.

According to Csikszentmihalyi, when people ponder further about what makes their lives rewarding, "they tend to move beyond pleasant memories and begin to remember other events, other experiences that overlap with pleasurable ones but fall into a category that deserves a separate name: *enjoyment*."[12] People describe themselves as experiencing enjoyment when they put the whole of themselves into an activity and go beyond where they were previously. "Playing a close game of tennis that stretches one's ability is enjoyable," he writes, "as is reading a book that reveals things in a new light, as is having a conversation that leads us to express ideas we didn't know we had."[13] After such activities, people find themselves saying "That was fun," or "That was enjoyable." Such experiences are also related to the growth of the person.[14]

ELEMENTS OF THE FLOW EXPERIENCE

During a flow experience the person centers his attention on a limited stimulus field; he is completely immersed in the activity. According to John Brodie, former San Francisco 49er quarterback, such immersion is needed to play sports well. As he puts it,

> A player's effectiveness is directly related to his ability to be right there, doing that thing, in the moment....He can't be worrying about the past or the future or the crowd or some extraneous event. He must be able to respond in the here and now.[15]

When a person is centering his attention on the task at hand, he experiences a "merging of action and awareness"; what he is doing and what he is thinking about have become one.[16]

During flow, the person forgets about himself temporarily, or experiences an "ego-lessness." This doesn't mean that the self disappears, but rather that explicit reflection on the self stops for the time being. Because the activity requires all the person's attention, he doesn't have attention remaining to be wondering "How am I doing?" "What do they think of me?" or "What will I get out of this?" As Csikszentmihalyi puts it, "The 'me' disappears during flow, and the 'I' takes over."[17]

The Joy of Playing Sports

Thoughts that explicitly take the self as an object of reflection interrupt flow. This can happen even when everything is going well. One high school basketball player described such a dynamic: "When I get hot in a game...like I said, you don't think about it at all. If you step back and think about why you are so hot all of a sudden you get creamed."[18] This element of the flow experience is intriguing, because it suggests that when a person is playing a sport at a high level, he isn't operating in an egocentric way. Indeed, egocentrism in this sense undermines his ability to play well.

While a person doesn't have attention to explicitly think of himself during flow, afterward when he does have such attention available, he is aware that his self has grown. According to Csikszentmihalyi, loss of self-consciousness and self-transcendence are related:

> When not preoccupied with ourselves, we actually have a chance to expand the concept of who we are. Loss of self-consciousness can lead to self-transcendence, to a feeling that the boundaries of our being have been pushed forward.[19]

The way people often describe such growth is that they are more aware of their individual skills and of being part of something larger than themselves, which leads to the next element: an experience of unity with one's surroundings. While climbing a mountain, a person may become more aware than usual of the beauty or grandeur that surrounds him and experience a new sense of connection to the natural environment. While playing lead guitar in a band, a person may experience a kind of attunement or being in sync with the bass player and drummer and rhythm guitarist. In team sports, players and coaches often mention the close bond that develops between the players, which develops in large part because they must work together to accomplish their goals. But the experience of unity among team members will only happen if the players can reach a point where they are no longer thinking in a self-centered way. As Phil Jackson puts it, "The struggle every group leader faces [is] how to get members of the team who are driven by the quest for individual glory to give themselves over wholeheartedly to the group effort. In other words, how to teach them selflessness."[20]

People who experience flow also describe an *effortlessness* to their action, as though they are being carried along by a current. This is the dimension of the experience that the word *flow* captures. But such ease or effortlessness is preceded by extensive experience and practice of the relevant skills in one's domain. When we are first learning any skill, it doesn't feel natural. And we have to think a lot about what we are doing and practice the skill over a long period of time. Consider a right-handed, sixth-grade basketball player who is learning how to shoot a layup with her left hand. She initially must think a great deal about what her coach tells her with respect to which foot to jump off, when to jump, the motion of her shooting hand, and so on. She has to practice the shot for many months. And she will make countless mistakes, miss shots, and probably have several run-ins with the garage door along the way! However, if she internalizes her coach's instructions and practices the layup over an extended period, when she receives a pass on a fast break on the left side of the court in eighth grade, she will be able to shoot the left-handed layup effortlessly, as though she has been doing it her whole life.

If a person is experiencing flow while playing a sport, he or she will also experience time differently. If this occurs while playing soccer at the school yard, several hours might pass by in what seems like a few minutes. The person might even forget to come home for lunch. On the other hand, sometimes during a flow experience time seems to slow down and something that took only a few seconds seems to have lasted much longer. This usually happens when the action is proceeding at a very fast pace and the player needs it to slow down in order to perform well. Several of my students who played baseball for the university team said that this happened when they were at bat, trying to hit a baseball that's coming in at over ninety miles per hour and changing directions in midstream.

LOVE AND RESPECT

According to Csikszentmihalyi, "Being human we all want, first of all, to survive, to be comfortable, to be accepted, loved and respected."[21] Such an experience of being loved and accepted provides a sense of security and helps to foster a sense of self that makes it possible for a young person to immerse himself in an enjoyable activity for its own sake. A young person who grows up in a home where there is neglect or abuse, on the other hand, will find it more difficult to have the kind of flow experiences that make life rewarding and contribute to his growth.

> It stands to reason...that a child who has been abused, or who has been often threatened with the withdrawal of parental love—and unfortunately we are becoming increasingly aware of what a disturbing proportion of children in our culture are so mistreated—will be so worried about keeping his sense of self from coming apart as to have little energy left to pursue intrinsic rewards.[22]

Other scholars have written about similar themes. In her article "Meanings of the Body," Lynne Belaief writes about the importance of an experience of "ontological security," which "includes not only a firm sense of one's own existence but of the *rightness* of that existence."[23] For Belaief, when ontologically secure, we can enter into experiences for their own sake: we can play.

CHARACTERISTICS OF FLOW ACTIVITIES

Activities that are conducive to flow also have distinctive characteristics. One characteristic is that the activity is usually challenging and requires skills. However, there needs to be a balance between the level of challenge and the person's own skill level. If the activity is too challenging, he will feel overwhelmed and anxious. On the other hand, if the activity is not challenging enough, he will feel bored and uninterested. Flow is experienced when the challenge is at the growing edge of a person's skill level.[24]

When I was growing up, we had a ping-pong table in the basement. The most enjoyable moments in the games were when the volleys back and forth were the longest. According to the flow theory, this is because at these times my companion and I were playing at the growing edge of our skill level. And we were pushing one another in that direction each time we returned a volley. This interpretation helps us to understand why youth sports contests between evenly matched teams can be so exhilarating. It also helps us to understand how participation in sport at elite and professional levels can still be enjoyable and intrinsically rewarding.

Flow activities also have clear goals and provide feedback. A basketball player knows that the goal is to put the ball in the basket, for example. If the player is practicing free throws, he or she can keep track of how many are successful out of twenty on successive days and in this way chart personal improvement or regression. The goal for a basketball team is to put the ball in the basket more often than their opponents, and this means they have the more complex tasks of working with one another by setting picks, running plays, and passing the ball so that they can be positioned to take good shots and collaborating to stop the opponents (without fouling or goaltending). Coaches facilitate a process by which individuals and the team can come up with goals and give regular feedback as the season is progressing in relation to how well they are doing in reaching these goals.

FLOW IS NOT AN ABSOLUTE GOOD

The fact that a person is experiencing flow does not tell us everything we need to know about the value of an activity, or the importance it should have in his or her life. A person might spend too much time on an activity in which they experience flow, to the neglect of other activities that are important to pay attention to, given the broader context of their life. Regarding youth sports, this can be an issue when high school students (usually because they think they have a future in elite-level sport) devote all their attention to sport to the neglect of their studies—or other formative experiences related to their holistic growth and development. Since so few young people actually earn a full college scholarship for sports or advance to play at the professional or elite level, the lack of attention to studies or other broadening formative experiences can leave many young people ill-equipped for the realities of life after school.

It is also possible to become addicted to a flow activity. People who do so may narrow their attention so much that they ignore other dimensions of their human experience, even those which are important for them to attend to for their growth as whole persons.

If athletic training and broader assumptions in the culture of a sport lead athletes to experience their bodies as a machine, this can also be related to their increasing distance from the affective dimension of their lives—especially when it comes to feelings that are painful or confusing. Unfortunately, some athletes only face these feelings, and themselves, later in life, usually after a personal crisis or even after causing harm to someone else or getting into trouble with the law.

Sometimes broader ethical criteria are needed to evaluate a particular context within which flow is experienced. Some of my students have written papers about how they experienced the elements of flow while in training exercises in the military, for example. And if they experienced these elements of flow, they very likely experienced personal growth. However, the flow experience itself and their personal growth tell us nothing about whether the war they will eventually fight is a just war. This requires a broader ethical analysis. In a similar vein, it is possible to experience flow while participating in sports where long term damage to the health of participants is possible or even likely. A broader ethical analysis is required in the case of some sports, then, to determine whether the flow experiences participants have while playing them lead to their well-being in a more holistic sense.

FLOW, SPORT, AND CHRISTIAN SPIRITUALITY

Several themes in Christian spirituality can be correlated with the experiences of flow in play and sport. One of the first that comes to mind is the recognition that we get off track when we become too attached to money and status. Throughout the Gospels, Jesus warns of the dangers of attachment to wealth, and he repeatedly reminds his followers not to be so concerned with their own status and honor.[25] Ignatius of Loyola writes in his Spiritual Exercises that it is characteristic of the one whom he calls the "enemy of our human nature" to ensnare people in the following way:

> People find themselves tempted to covet whatever seems to make them rich, and next because they possess some thing or things they find themselves pursuing and basking in the honor and esteem of this world. Then getting such deference raises up the false sense of personal identity and value in which a blinding pride has its roots.[26]

Ignatius is identifying a dynamic that he says can "ensnare" people; it is associated with disorder and dysfunction, both in our personal lives and in human societies.

The flow experience is intriguing because people who are experiencing flow have interior freedom with respect to money and status. They have discovered the intrinsic meaning and rewards of what they are doing. The music composer we quoted earlier expressed this succinctly:

PLAY, SPORT, AND SPIRIT

> One doesn't do it for *money*....This is what I tell my students. Don't expect to make *money*, don't expect *fame* or a *pat on the back*, don't expect a damn thing. Do it because you love it.[27]

According to Csikszentmihalyi, a young person is more able to enter into an activity for its intrinsic rewards when he knows that he is loved and accepted. And this is why growing up in a loving and supportive environment is so important. Belaief writes about the importance of having a sense of "ontological security," which enables a person to play in freedom. Their reflections call to mind what Burghardt said about the importance of a "relaxed field" for play.

Philosopher William Sadler explains the connection for human beings between the experience of being loved and being able to play. He points out that "as animals must have a sense of security to really play, so men [*sic*] must have a sense of being loved."

> In the heart of man there is a longing for loving encounter in which one's freedom will be acknowledged and affirmed. In order to play most creatively one needs to develop a sense of trust not merely in himself or in the other, but basically in the world which opens before him. This is precisely the world which love provides. Love gives man a home in which it is safe to play.[28]

Sadler draws on Huizinga's *Homo Ludens*, as well as contemporary psychiatric studies, that help us understand that the "playground of freedom is love....It is a gift of trust, an embrace which affirms the significance of the individual and the importance of becoming himself in a common world. Freedom does not die in love; it is born there."[29]

The importance of a person knowing that he or she is loved and this leading to freedom is also a central theme in Christian spirituality. According to St. Paul, love is the paramount reality in the Christian life. Even if a person has faith that can move mountains, or spiritual gifts such as speaking in tongues, these mean nothing if he does not have love; in such cases, the person is merely a "noisy gong" or a "clanging cymbal" (1 Cor 13:1). Jesus tells his followers, "As the Father has loved me, so I have loved you; abide in my love" (John 15:9). And he exhorts them to love one another. Some contemporary theologians point out that a person who has experienced God's love and remains in this love has a sense of "ontological security" and hence has the freedom to play. As the Jesuit Hugo Rahner puts it, "[The person] who has faith and truly loves God is also the [one] who can truly play, for only he who is secure in God can be truly light of heart."[30]

UNION WITH ONE'S SURROUNDINGS

Does love have any relevance in a highly competitive athletic milieu? There is some evidence that it does. Catholic high school football coach and theology teacher Bob Ladouceur guided his De La Salle (Concord, California) team to twelve consecutive undefeated seasons from 1992 to 2004, setting a national record for consecutive wins. Yet Coach Ladouceur doesn't talk much about winning. However, he does talk a good deal about the love his players and coaches have for one another. As he puts it,

PLAY, SPORT, AND SPIRIT

> We try to make our football team a safe place to be. Safe to be our self. There is nowhere to hide on a football field. Teammates know each other, coaches know the players, and the players know the coaches. All attempts at not being yourself fail miserably. The key is to be the best self you were created to be. We work hard at breaking down the walls that separate us called race, status, religion, jealousy, hate and culture—and truly experience each other on a purely human level....Our founder, St. John Baptist De La Salle, says that the spirit of our Lasallian family is a spirit of faith and ardent zeal. And that the motivating force of zeal is love.[31]

According to Ladouceur, at De La Salle they don't measure success in wins and titles. "It's what got us those titles that we are most proud of....What beats at the heart of our neighborhood is love. Yes, we win because our players love each other. They are not afraid to say it or embrace each other as a sign of that affection." Speaking from the point of view of a player, he says, "Wherever I go or whatever I do, I carry my team with me knowing full well that I am connected to a group that loves, accepts, and respects me."[32]

Ladouceur's emphasis on the young men being known and knowing the other players and coaches corresponds well with what Jesuit scientist Pierre Teilhard de Chardin says about the experience of union with another person or persons that is rooted in love. Such a union does not require a person to abandon his true self or identity, as can happen with young people who join gangs or when people get caught up in a personality cult around a political or religious leader. For Chardin, the experience of genuine union with another person or persons in love leads to the *discovery* of oneself. As he puts it, "Union differentiates." For human beings, however, "to become truly personalized under the creative influence of union, they must not be joined haphazardly. Since it is actually a question of creating a synthesis of centers, they must enter into mutual contact center to center, and *in no other way*."[33] And it is love that brings about such mutual contact: "Love alone is capable of completing our beings in themselves as it unites them, for the good reason that love alone takes them and joins them by their very depths."[34]

FLOW, SPORT, AND THE REST OF THE SPIRITUAL LIFE

Csikszentmihalyi recognizes that sometimes athletes who experience flow while playing their sport experience meaninglessness and dissolution in the rest of their lives. The same is true of artists and others. For this reason, he was interested in mining the resources of the flow research for insights into how all aspects of a person's life could be made more meaningful. In this next section, I will be making some connections between the dynamics of the flow experience and the dynamics of the Christian life in a general sense, drawing on the insights of Ignatius of Loyola.

Some of the major themes in Ignatius's spirituality are analogous to themes expressed in the literature on the flow experience. It is an understatement to say that Ignatius was single-minded. After his leg was shattered by a cannonball at Pamplona and he had his eye-and-heart opening experiences while convalescing, he lived the rest of his life with the intention of having everything he did devoted purely to the service, honor, and praise of God. "The eye of our intention," he wrote, "ought to be single."[35] His Spiritual Exercises retreat provides a context within which people can discern how to live their lives and make choices in a way that flow "from the love of God" and hence are "for the greater glory of God" and service of others.[36]

As was mentioned earlier, the purpose of the Spiritual Exercises retreat is to help a person arrive at interior freedom so he can recognize and respond to God's love and call in his life. And so, the retreat provides opportunities for the person to consider where he might have "inordinate attachments" or "disordered affections."[37] We have already seen how attachments to money, fame, or what others think of us can interfere with our ability to play games well. Attachments can also be disruptive in our life in general. The common feature of our attachments is that they keep us from being free enough to say "Yes" to what God is doing in the world and in our lives, which leads to new life for ourselves and others.

JOY

As was discussed in the previous chapter, for Ignatius when a person is growing in the Christian life, one important way that he has a sense of how God is acting in his life is through the experience of spiritual consolation. Ignatius's description of spiritual consolation is analogous to Csikszentmihalyi's description of the flow experience. Such consolation is associated with "genuine happiness and spiritual joy," for example.[38] Joy is very important in the scriptures and for Jesus himself. The reign of God was the central theme of Jesus's life and preaching. The parables he uses to describe it highlight the reality of God's *overflowing* love, abundance, and superfluity.[39] In one parable, Jesus compares the reign of God to a treasure buried in a field. When a person finds this treasure, "out of joy" he sells all that he has to buy the field (Matt 13:44). For Jesus, then, the motivation for his life and work and that of his followers, including leaving behind or selling all one owns, is the joy associated with the discovery of the reign of God.[40]

EFFORTLESSNESS

As mentioned in the previous chapter, Ignatius also described the experience of spiritual consolation as effortless. He says it feels gentle and easy, "like water going into a sponge" or like "coming into one's own house through an open door." Such an experience of consolation may just happen—without previous cause. But as is the case in flow experiences, it is usually preceded by disciplined attention and practice. Ignatius's retreat is called the Spiritual *Exercises*, after all. During the retreat, the person spends time "considering" certain themes and "reflecting" on his life, doing imaginative prayer with the gospel accounts of the life of Christ, and engaging in other prayer exercises. Some of these exercises invite the person toward greater freedom from attachments so they can experience God's love and respond to the leading and promptings of the Spirit. These promptings will be recognized as coming from the Holy Spirit because they are experienced as "coming home" to oneself and one's place in the world effortlessly, as though "by an open door."[41]

EGOLESSNESS

When a person is experiencing spiritual consolation, she has a felt sense of being in God's presence and an awareness that she is part of something much larger than herself. She may have new ideas about how to help others and energy to carry these ideas out. Her attention is on meeting the challenges involved in her work and on service to others, not on herself. In this sense, the experience is egoless.[42] According to Beatrice Bruteau, when a person has the experience of God working in and through her, she is egoless:

> We not only do not take pride in what we do, we are scarcely aware of ourselves as the ones who are doing. We do not reflect upon ourselves in order to *observe that* we are leaving ourselves open to God's work and that such and so is taking place through us. We simply open ourselves and let our whole awareness be of God's life in and through us to whatever the work or expression of divine beauty and goodness is. The more we can make our eye "single" in this way and not let it divide into a double consciousness—partly on God's act of living and working through us, and partly a reflection on how well we're doing—the more our whole being, like the crystal, will be filled with the divine light.
>
> In this way we gradually come to renounce our most fundamental habits of self-consciousness.[43]

Bruteau points out that when God is working through a person and there is fruit in her ministry, there is always the temptation to redirect her attention to herself, just as the high school basketball player did when he was playing so well. When she can resist this and make her "eye single," however, God's love can more easily flow through her to others.

FROM GOOD TO BETTER

Since flow and spiritual consolation share many similarities, it is probably not surprising to learn that they are both related to the growth and development of the person. As Ignatius put it, "The good angel acts for the progress of the soul, that it may grow and rise from what is good to what is better."[44] And Pope Francis recently told the Jesuits that "in the *Exercises*, progress in the spiritual life is made through consolation: it is a moving from good to better as well as 'every increase of hope, faith, and charity.'"[45]

Spiritual consolation is broader than what has been studied to date in flow research. As has been mentioned in earlier footnotes, it can be experienced in forgiveness and reconciliation or in the midst of suffering and loss. Still, the flow research is very important because it helps us connect the dots between many of our experiences in daily life and spiritual consolation. Some flow experiences may be analogous to spiritual consolation, but not spiritual consolation *per se*. Other flow experiences are themselves experiences of spiritual consolation. Indeed, what we are learning about the complementarity of flow experiences and spiritual consolation may help us understand in a new way how "grace perfects nature."[46]

FLOW, SPIRITUAL CONSOLATION, AND YOUNG ATHLETES

The analogies between flow and spiritual consolation suggest that the flow experiences young people have in sport can have significance for their lives long after they are done playing. This is very important for college student athletes, who often come to view their participation in sport as central to their identity. It is not uncommon for them to have problems adjusting and making a transition to a meaningful life and vocation after their playing days are over. I experienced this myself after my college football-playing days were over when I was in my twenties.

In their flow experiences in sport, student athletes have a helpful resource as they pivot to the rest of their lives. They don't have to turn their backs completely on the sport they loved playing all through their youth. Rather, they can pay attention to where the elements of flow they experienced playing sports are present in their current experience as they study different subjects, consider majors, or engage in volunteer or work projects. This kind of reflection can help them to make decisions about their major and the kind of work they want to do.

Madison, a student athlete at the University of Detroit Mercy, was helped by studying flow to see a "through line" from her soccer playing to her future career as a nurse. She wrote in a paper that when she was thinking about a career "nothing felt like a better fit" than nursing because it was about helping people "in their weakest, most vulnerable state" and giving them "care, comfort, support, and love." As she put it,

> Just as when I play soccer I am able to completely immerse myself into a zone where no outside distractions affect me, I also see myself getting lost in a process I enjoy when I become a nurse and have to take care of people. I can build this new flow experience upon my older one because of the way I know and understand myself. When I am taking care of others, I forget about what I need at that moment. The only thing I am focused on are the needs of the person I

am helping and how I can attempt to alleviate their suffering. This directly relates to several different sensations I experience when I play soccer. When I am playing with my team, I put their needs on the field before my own so that we can accomplish the greater goal we all share. I put aside my own wants and needs and look at the bigger picture of my team.

Reflecting on how my current experience of flow will be a foundation for my future career as a nurse was quite eye-opening to me. I am extremely grateful that I know the occupation I have chosen to pursue will be the right fit for me as it will also give me a daily flow experience so that I do not lose this important element from my life when I move on from college and no longer play soccer.

In other reflections during the semester, Madison described experiencing spiritual consolation as she engaged in her studies and provided care for patients in their moments of vulnerability and need. These experiences of spiritual consolation helped confirm her decision to major in nursing.

Other student athletes find it helpful to reflect on current flow experiences in their studies, volunteering, and work when making decisions about their future, but don't refer explicitly to Ignatius's spiritual consolation. This may be because they don't consider themselves religious or spiritual or because they belong to a different religious tradition than Ignatius did. However, the insights they have gained by reflecting on their flow experiences open the door to the possibility of their reflecting in the future on the spiritual dimension of their life experiences in the context of their own faith stance and worldview.

Flow experiences, then, help us to understand the human and potential spiritual significance of playing sport. It is crucially important that the sport be engaged in for its own sake and have its own meaning. So, this is not an instrumental approach in the usual sense. The significance of flow experiences for life in the future has to do with the fact that the young person knows what it feels like to engage in an activity that has internal goods and is *intrinsically* valued. As Madison put it, "Flow seems to be the result of an experience that one finds to be intrinsically rewarding; the lack of external pushes to become engaged in an activity allows [people] to fully immerse themselves in whatever they are doing so that they are able to 'get lost' in the process and find true satisfaction with it."

Flow experiences young people have while playing sports tell them something important about themselves and what they long for: joy that is experienced as they immerse themselves in meaningful activities with intrinsic rewards, the opportunity to use and develop their gifts selflessly in the service of something larger than themselves, the experience of love and friendship with other people and a sense of unity with all of creation. In this sense they are "signals of transcendence" and point to what will provide meaning and joy in the rest of their lives as well.[47]

CONCLUSION

JOHAN HUIZINGA WROTE already in the 1930s that the "old play-factor [had] undergone almost complete atrophy" in modern sport. Because of this, he thought that modern sport was no longer a "culture-creating activity," but rather had become "sterile." Indeed, in his view modern sport "occupies a place alongside and apart from the cultural process."[1]

For Huizinga, play is related to culture in that it reminds us that we are free, that we don't live by bread alone. It is a *significant* activity and has meaning. Play contributes to the well-being of the group, but in ways that are different from the satisfaction of material needs or necessities. One of the ways sport in earlier periods was part of the cultural process was that it was tied to religious festivals and so had a "higher significance."

> The great competitions in ancient cultures had always formed part of the sacred festivals and were indispensable as health- and happiness-bringing activities. This ritual tie has now been completely severed; sport has become profane, "unholy" in every way.[2]

PLAY, SPORT, AND SPIRIT

For Huizinga, then, the atrophy of the play factor in modern sport was related to its losing its cultural and spiritual significance.

Huizinga's reflections have relevance for our contemporary context where the play element of sport has been even more marginalized than in his time. If what he says is true about the relationship between play, culture, and spirituality, it would make sense that the "atrophying of the play factor" is part of what has made it so difficult for us to understand the relationship between sport and spirituality in our own context. On the other hand, if we were able to give a "thick description" of the play element of sport, this could be a very helpful resource for understanding the relationship between sport and spirituality today. This has been demonstrated to be true in this book.

But to engage in this kind of project is to go against long and deep cultural trends in the United States. Because of the Puritan work ethic, the subsequent rise of industrialization, and other factors, Americans throughout much of our early history exalted work, associating it with "godliness," and tended to regard play with suspicion, even associating it with sin. This is related to the trend toward instrumental thinking in our context that has led us to neglect or overlook the importance of enjoyment in play and doing something for its own sake. This instrumental thinking is heightened by the recent emergence of a "market society," in which sport has become increasingly regarded as a means to attaining external goods such as money, fame, institutional prestige, and so on.

In earlier periods we have seen that certain sociocultural phenomena and theological influences supported the play element of sport. For example, in the late medieval and early modern periods sports were played on feast days, during which "ordinary life [was] at a standstill."[3] These feast days provided a

Conclusion

formal boundary that protected them from the intrusion of concerns about work and the practical concerns of everyday life. Theologians also took play seriously and argued for its importance in human life. In the thirteenth century, Thomas Aquinas argued that there could be a virtue about play and games on the grounds that virtue had to do with moderation. Working all the time would be immoderate; thus, a fully human life also needed time for play and recreation. For Aquinas, playful activities are autotelic, and yet have benefits. As he put it, actions done playfully, "are not directed to any external end; but merely to the good of the [player], in so far as they afford him pleasure or relaxation."[4] This "play ethic" influenced Western cultural traditions and education up through the nineteenth century in the United States. While some Catholic philosophers and theologians kept this ethic alive in their writings in the late nineteenth and twentieth centuries, they did not turn their attention to sport itself in a sustained way. This has meant that the implications of the play ethic for sport have not yet been adequately developed.

In this book the research and reflections of Gordon Burghardt, Randolph Feezell, and Mihaly Csikszentmihalyi have helped us to develop these implications. In particular, they have helped us understand how play can be autotelic and yet have benefits for the player in our own context. The five criteria Gordon Burghardt provided for identifying play include that the activity (1) has limited immediate functional value (it includes elements that don't contribute to survival), (2) is pleasurable and done for its own sake, (3) is different from the way it would be carried out in ordinary life, (4) is performed repeatedly at some point in the life span, and (5) is initiated in the security provided by a "relaxed field." He pointed out that animal—including human—play is most prevalent when there are surplus resources or abundance. He also introduced the notion of primary process play, which is made possible by fortuitous conditions, and pointed out that such play itself does not have any purpose. Once such play exists, however, it may evolve some role in the development of physiological and behavioral capacities in secondary play or in enhancing behavioral capacities, "including the development of innovation and creativity" in tertiary play.[5]

Cardinal Ratzinger understands contemporary sport in an analogous way. For him, sport is an experience of play engaged in freely and without a purpose, and yet it provides a "training for life." In his view, it is precisely this both/and quality that gives sport its appeal. We have seen that when sport is *played*, it can indeed enrich human life and lead to the growth of the person. The writings of Feezell have helped us understand how *playing* sport is related to the person experiencing freedom and expressing his true self. When a person experiences flow in sport, he enjoys what he is doing for its own sake, is selfless, and has an experience of being part of something larger than himself. He grows as a person in this process.

Burghardt's point about the importance of surplus resources and being in a relaxed field in order for play to occur finds an intriguing analogy in Jesus's teaching about the reign of God. According to this teaching, God's abundant and overflowing love is at the heart of the human experience of the reign of God. The experience of "salvation," in this sense, has to do with abundance, excess, and superfluity. As scripture scholar Gerhard Lohfink puts it,

> Superfluity, wealth, and extravagant luxury are thus the signs of the day of salvation—not skimpiness, meagerness, wretchedness, and need. Why? Because God's very self is overflowing life and because God longs to give a share in that life. God's love is without measure;

Conclusion

God does not give to human beings according to the measure of their own good behavior or service.[6]

According to Lohfink, this abundance and superfluity can be discerned in creation itself.

> The principle of superfluity is already revealed in creation. Biologists have long since observed that quantitative and qualitative extravagance plays a striking role in nature, and that evolution cannot be fully explained by a calculus of usefulness. Nature is "luxuriant."[7]

Lohfink's reflections find support in scripture. According to the Psalmist, it is because God cares and provides for the earth so abundantly that creation itself is "luxuriant."

> The ends of the earth stand in awe
>   at the sight of your wonders.
> The lands of sunrise and sunset
>   you fill with your joy.
>
> You care for the earth, give it water;
>   you *fill it with riches*.
> Your river in heaven *brims over*
>   to provide its grain.
>
> And thus you provide for the earth;
>   you *drench its furrows*,
> you level it, soften it with showers,
>   you bless its growth.

PLAY, SPORT, AND SPIRIT

For the Psalmist, God's goodness is the source of the abundance that *flows* into creation in such a way that makes even the hills, meadows, and valleys rejoice.

> You crown the year with your goodness.
> *Abundance flows in your steps,*
> *in the pastures of the wilderness it flows.*
>
> The hills are girded with joy,
>   the meadows covered with flocks,
> the valleys are decked with wheat.
>   They shout for joy, yes they sing.[8]

Pope Francis thinks *overflow* is an ideal term for capturing Jesus's teaching about who God is and what God is doing in the world. He explains,

> "Overflow" is one possible translation of the Greek *perisseuo*, which is the word used by the psalmist whose cup overflows with God's grace in Psalm 23. *Perissueo* was what Jesus promises (Luke 6:38) will be poured into our laps when we forgive. It is the noun deployed in John's Gospel (John 10:10) to describe the life that Jesus came to bring, and the adjective Saint Paul uses (2 Corinthians 1:5) to describe God's generosity. It is the very heart of God that overflows in those famous passages of the father rushing out to hug his prodigal son, the wedding host who gathers guests from the roads and the fields for his banquet, the net-breaking catch of fish at dawn after a night of fruitless trawling, or Jesus washing the feet of his disciples on the night before he died. Such overflows of love happen, above all, at the

Conclusion

crossroads of life, at moments of openness, fragility, and humility, when the ocean of His love bursts the dams of our self-sufficiency, and so allows for a new imagination of the possible.[9]

To say "Yes" to God, whose very self is "overflowing life," is also to grow in freedom. In this sense, the dynamics associated with the evolution of animal play as described by Burghardt are analogous to the dynamics of spiritual growth in human beings. When the animal is safe in an environment of parental care (a relaxed field) and surplus resources are available, the selection of narrowly channeled instinctual drives is relaxed and the animal experiences increased flexibility or plasticity. They are open to learning new things from experience. This is a context within which their more generalized set of capacities can develop.

In the Spiritual Exercises retreat of Ignatius it is crucial to begin with an existential awareness of being in the relaxed field of God's love and care. And the growth of the person in freedom and flexibility happens as a consequence of the "felt knowledge" of this love deepening. Like other animals, human beings are influenced/shaped by biological (instinctual) factors and in our case cultural factors as well. We can become stuck in the pursuit of biological pleasures, or we can uncritically let cultural scripts for what is of value in life influence us in such a way that we lose touch with the deeper wellsprings of our existence, which are rooted in God. The purpose of the Spiritual Exercises is to help the person move to greater freedom from the determining influences of genes/culture, which allows them to be open to learning something new based on their own lived experiences of life and prayer. Something called "indifference" is important to Ignatius because it signals flexibility to move in one direction or the other depending on how the Spirit is leading. One theologian describes this as being like a good shortstop, who is ready to move at the crack of the bat. Such freedom allows the person to walk more closely with Jesus in the Spirit, so that more and more of their life becomes a yes to God's abundant love and mercy that overflows into all of God's creation.

NOTES

PREFACE

1. Johan Huizinga, *Homo Ludens: A Study of the Play Element in Culture* (Boston: Beacon Press, 1955).

2. Mihaly Csikszentmihalyi, *FLOW: The Psychology of Optimal Experience* (New York: Harper and Row, 1990).

3. Mihaly Csikszentmihalyi, *Beyond Boredom and Anxiety: The Experience of Play in Work and Games* (San Francisco: Jossey-Bass, 1975), 37.

4. One of the reasons Csikszentmihalyi's research was so groundbreaking was because it provided a potential "through line" from experiences of play and other autotelic activities (and later, work) to experiences of transcendence as these have been described by spiritual writers in different religious traditions. It also made possible a new kind of dialogue, rooted in lived experiences, between members of different religious/spiritual traditions. I make use of the flow experience as a starting point to bring the ancient Chinese spiritual notion of *wu-wei* into dialogue with Ignatius of Loyola's "spiritual consolation" in Patrick Kelly, "Flow, Sport and Spiritual Traditions," in *Sport and Christianity: Practices for the Twenty-First Century*, ed. M. Hoven, A. Parker, and N. J. Watson (London: T & T Clark, 2020).

5. Patrick Kelly, *Catholic Perspectives on Sports: From Medieval to Modern Times*, esp. chaps. 2 and 4 (Mahwah, NJ: Paulist Press, 2012).

6. Aquinas, *Summa Theologica*, II–II, Q. 168, art. 4, trans. Fathers of the English Dominican Province (New York: Benziger Brothers, 1947).

7. *Thomas Aquinas: Summa Theologica*, I–II, Q. 1, art. 6, ad. 1, trans. Fathers of the English Dominican Province (New York: Benziger Brothers, 1947).

8. See Alessandra Rizzi, "Regulated Play at the End of the Middle Ages: The Work of Mendicant Preachers in Communal Italy," in *Sport and Culture in Early Modern Europe*, ed. John McClelland and Brian Merrilees (Toronto: Centre for Reformation and Renaissance Studies, 2010).

9. Kelly, *Catholic Perspectives on Sports*, esp. chaps. 2 and 5.

10. Michael J. Sandel, *What Money Can't Buy: The Moral Limits of Markets* (New York: Farrar, Strauss and Giroux, 2012).

11. Gordon M. Burghardt, *The Genesis of Animal Play: Testing the Limits* (Cambridge, MA: Massachusetts Institute of Technology, 2005).

12. Randolph Feezell, *Sport, Play, and Ethical Reflection* (Chicago: University of Illinois Press, 2006).

13. Mihaly Csikszentmihalyi, *Beyond Boredom and Anxiety: The Experience of Play in Work and Games* (San Francisco: Jossey-Bass, 1975).

14. Pope John Paul II, *Laborem Exercens: On Human Work* (1981). See par. 12, https://www.vatican.va/content/john-paul-ii/en/encyclicals/documents/hf_jp-ii_enc_14091981_laborem-exercens.html.

15. John Paul II, *Laborem Exercens*, pars. 6 and 9 passim.

CHAPTER 1

1. Josef Pieper, *Leisure: The Basis of Culture* (South Bend, IN: St. Augustine's Press, 1998), 22.

2. The full quote from Orwell is: "Serious sport has nothing to do with fair play. It is bound up with hatred, jealousy, boastfulness, disregard of all rules and sadistic pleasure in witnessing violence: In other words, it is war minus the shooting" ("The Sporting Spirit," in *Tribune*, London, December 1945). For a helpful discussion and critique of interpretations of ancient Greek athletics inspired by Orwell's understanding of sport, see Daniel A. Dombrowski, *Contemporary Athletics and Ancient Greek Ideals* (Chicago: The University of Chicago Press, 2009), 30ff.

Notes

3. Randolph Feezell, *Sport, Play, and Ethical Reflection* (Urbana: University of Illinois Press, 2004), 13.

4. See, e.g., Vern Seefeldt, Martha Ewing, and Stephan Walk, *Overview of Youth Sports Programs in the United States* (Washington, DC: Carnegie Council on Adolescent Development, 1993); Ryan Hedstrom and Daniel Gould, "Research in Youth Sports: Critical Issues Status" (East Lansing, MI: Institute for the Study of Youth Sports, 2004); Peggy McCann and Martha Ewing, "Motivation and Outcomes of Youth Participation in Sport," in *Learning Culture Through Sports: Exploring the Role of Sports in Society*, ed. Sandra Spickard Prettyman and Brian Lampman (Lanham, MD: Rowman & Littlefield, 2006); Amanda J. Visek, Sara M. Achrati, Heather M. Mannix, Karen McDonnell, Brandonn S. Harris, and Loretta DiPietro, "The Fun Integration Theory: Toward Sustaining Children and Adolescents Sport Participation," *Journal of Physical Activity and Health* 12, no. 3 (March 2015): 424–33.

5. L. J. Micheli and J. D. Klein, "Sports Injuries in Children and Adolescents," *British Journal of Sports Medicine* 25, no. 1 (March 1, 1991): 6–9; A. Ross Outerbridge and Lyle J. Micheli, "Adolescent Sports Medicine: Changing Patterns of Injury in the Young Athlete," *Sports Medicine and Arthroscopy Review* 4, no. 2 (Summer 1996): 93–98; Jennie McKee, "The Changing Landscape of Youth Sports Injuries," *AAOS Now*, American Academy of Orthopaedic Surgeons, November 2009; Joel S. Brenner, "Sports Specialization and Intensive Training in Young Athletes," *Pediatrics* 138, no. 3 (September 2016); John P. DiFiori, Holly J. Benjamin, Joel Brenner, Andrew Gregory, Neeru Jayanthi, Greg L. Landry, and Anthony Luke, "Overuse Injuries and Burnout in Youth Sports: A Position Statement from the American Medical Society for Sports Medicine," *Clinical Journal of Sport Medicine* 24, no. 1 (January 2014): 3–20; Bill Pennington, "Doctors See a Big Rise in Overuse Injuries for Young Athletes," *New York Times*, February 22, 2005; Mark Hyman, *Until It Hurts: America's Obsession with Youth Sports and How it Harms Our Kids* (Boston: Beacon Press, 2009).

6. Quoted in Bill Pennington, "As Team Sports Conflict, Some Parents Rebel," *New York Times*, November 12, 2003, https://www.nytimes.com/2003/11/12/sports/as-team-sports-conflict-some-parents-rebel.html.

7. Jay Coakley, "Sport Specialization and Its Effects," in *Learning Culture Through Sports: Perspectives on Society and Organized Sports*, ed. Brian Lampman and Sandra Spickard Prettyman, 2nd ed. (Lanham, MD: Rowman and Littlefield Publishers, 2011), 13; See also Jay Coakley, "The Logic of Specialization: Using Children for Adult Purposes," *Journal of Physical Education, Recreation & Dance* 81, no. 8 (October 2010).

8. See Hedstrom and Gould, "Research in Youth Sports: Critical Issues Status," 22–23; McCann and Ewing, "Motivation and Outcomes of Youth Participation in Sport," 38; V. Seefeld, M. Ewing, and S. Walk, *Overview of Youth Sports Programs*, 62–64; Peter A. Witt and Tek B. Dangi, "Why Children/Youth Drop Out of Sports," *Journal of Park and Recreation Administration* 36 (2018): 191–99; Youth in other countries also cite lack of fun or enjoyment as the main reason for dropping out of sport. See Jeff Crane and Viviene Temple, "A Systematic Review of Dropout from Organized Sport among Children and Youth," *European Physical Education Review* 21, no. 1 (February 2015): 114–31; Janice Butcher, Koenraad J. Lindner, and David P. Johns, "Withdrawal from Competitive Youth Sport: A Retrospective Ten-year Study," *Journal of Sport Behavior* 25, no. 2 (June 2002); Ronald Bishop expresses concern with the increasingly over-organized and supervised character of youth sports, which he claims squelches the play element: *When Play Was Play: Why Pickup Games Matter* (Albany: State University of New York Press, 2009).

9. Robert D. Putnam, *Our Kids: The American Dream in Crisis* (New York: Simon and Schuster, 2015), 174–83; Mark Hyman, *The Most Expensive Game in Town: The Rising Cost of Youth Sports and the Toll on Today's Families* (Boston: Beacon Press, 2012).

10. For a story about the rules violations of the successful Bellevue High School football program in Seattle, see Mike Baker, "Bellevue Football Report: Coaches Violated Rules for Years, District Obstructed Investigation," *Seattle Times*, May 26, 2016, https://www.seattletimes.com/sports/high-school/bellevue-football-report-finds-coaches-violated-rules-for-years-district-obstructed-investigation/.

11. According to William J. Morgan, this is because these theorists are "radically instrumentalist," that is, they view sport merely as an instrument of capitalism. In their view games and sport cannot "be

separated from the purposes to which they are put." William J. Morgan, *Leftist Theories of Sport: A Critique and Reconstruction* (Urbana: University of Illinois Press, 1994), 47. According to Morgan, they "take no account of the nature of sport," which for him consists in its "gratuitous manner" that distinguishes it from the rest of ordinary life (44).

12. This situation has analogies with a debate that Augustine had with the Manicheans in the fifth century. He was critical of their view that evil was inherent in the nature of things and their tendency to see sin everywhere. He pointed out that in order to understand what sin is, one must know what human nature is, because sin is "contrary to nature." As he put it, "A defect is against nature, because it harms a nature, and it would not harm it if it did not lessen its goodness. Therefore, evil is only a privation of good. Thus it never exists except in some good thing...." ("Answer to an Enemy of the Law and Prophets," in *Arianism and Other Heresies*, ed. John E. Rotelle, trans. and notes Roland J. Teske, Works of Saint Augustine: A Translation for the 21st Century, part 1, vol. 18 [New York: New City Press, 1995], 360–61.) Likewise, in our context in order to understand the "defects" or corruption of sport, we must understand what sport is and what the internal goods are associated with its practice (without necessarily having to regard sport as having a "nature" or "essence" that is independent of historical, social, and cultural context).

13. Some philosophers of sport have been making use of the notion of sport as a social practice to understand sport and its relationship to other aspects of society. Drawing on the writings of Alisdair MacIntyre, these philosophers understand sport as a social practice that has internal ends or goods and is embedded in a historical context and tradition. Sport practices are vulnerable to corruption by the desire for external goods, which he says institutions are characteristically interested in. And virtue is required of practitioners to protect the internal goods of the sport. With regard to other domains of culture being instrumentalized in pursuit of external goods, see, e.g., Michael J. Sandel, *What Money Can't Buy: The Moral Limits of Markets* (New York: Farrar, Straus and Giroux, 2012); Martha C. Nussbaum, *Not for Profit: Why Democracy Needs the Humanities* (Princeton, NJ: Princeton University Press, 2010); William Deresiewicz, *Excellent Sheep: The Miseducation of the American Elite and the Way to a Meaningful Life* (New York: Free Press, 2014); Jackson Lears, "A Place and Time Apart: The Liberal Arts

vs. Neoliberalism," *Commonweal* 142, no. 8 (May 1, 2015): 14–21; Eric Bennett, "Dear Humanities Profs: We Are the Problem," *Chronicle of Higher Education*, April 13, 2018.

14. Huizinga first published this book in Dutch in 1938, with the title *Homo ludens: Proeve eener bepaling van het spel-element der cultuur* (Groningen: Wolters-Noordhoff, 1938). It was translated into German in 1944 and first translated into English in 1949 as *Homo Ludens: A Study of the Play Element in Culture* (London: Routledge and Kegan Paul, 1949). For the footnotes in this book, I am using the edition published by Johan Huizinga, *Homo Ludens: A Study of the Play Element in Culture* (Boston: Beacon Press, 1955).

15. Huizinga, *Homo Ludens*, 2.

16. Huizinga, *Homo Ludens*, 2–3.

17. Huizinga, *Homo Ludens*, 3.

18. Huizinga, *Homo Ludens*, 4.

19. Articles on play are rare in academic journals dealing with spirituality. The only article with the word *play* in the title for the journal *Spiritus: A Journal of Christian Spirituality* is Patricia Beckman's "Swimming in the Trinity: Mechthild of Magdeburg's Dynamic Play," *Spiritus* 4, no. 1 (Spring 2004). When the term *play* is searched for as content it doesn't bring up much more. The first several entries after Beckman's article are poems which merely contain the word *play*. The Jesuit journal *The Way: Review of Contemporary Christian Spirituality*, which published an issue titled "Humor and Play," *The Way* 31, no. 3 (1991), seems to be an exception in this regard.

20. The Puritans were more suspicious of play and recreation than either Martin Luther or John Calvin were. See Patrick Kelly, *Catholic Perspectives on Sports* (Mahwah, NJ: Paulist Press, 2012), 14ff.

21. Richard Baxter, *A Christian Directory, or a Summa of Practical Theology and Cases of Conscience*, vol. 2 (London: Printed for Richard Edwards, 1825), 618–19.

22. Quoted in William Hogan, "Sin and Sport," in *Motivations in Play, Games and Sports*, ed. Slovenko and Knight (Springfield, IL: Thomas, 1967), 124–25. Italics in original.

23. Victor Turner, "Liminal to Liminoid, in Play, Flow, and Ritual: An Essay in Comparative Symbology," *Rice University Studies* 60, no. 3

Notes

(Summer 1974): 66. See also Keith Thomas, "Work and Leisure in Pre-Industrial Society," *Past & Present* 29, no. 1 (December 1964): 50–62.

24. For one philosopher's take on how the repression of play led to the instrumentalization of sport in the American context, see William J. Morgan, "Play, Utopia, and Dystopia: Prologue to a Ludic Theory of the State," *Journal of the Philosophy of Sport* 9, no. 1 (1982): 30–42; in recent years other scholars have emphasized the human and cultural significance of play in light of what they perceive to be a repression and marginalization of play in U.S. culture. See, e.g., Diane Ackerman, *Deep Play* (New York: Random House, 1999); Stuart Brown with Christopher Vaughan, *Play: How It Shapes the Brain, Opens the Imagination and Invigorates the Soul* (New York: Penguin, 2009); Alan Lightman, *In Praise of Wasting Time* (New York: Simon and Schuster, 2018), see esp. chap. 4, "Play"; Martha C. Nussbaum, *Not for Profit: Why Democracy Needs the Humanities* (Princeton, NJ: Princeton University Press, 2010), esp. chap. 6; Pasi Sahlberg and William Doyle, *Let the Children Play: How More Play Will Save Our Schools and Help Children Thrive* (New York: Oxford University Press, 2019); Stephen T. Asma, "Reclaiming the Power of Play," *New York Times*, April 27, 2015; Pasi Sahlberg and William Doyle, "To Really Learn, Our Children Need the Power of Play," *Wall Street Journal*, August 8, 2019.

25. Michael J. Sandel, *What Money Can't Buy: The Moral Limits of Markets* (New York: Farrar, Strauss and Giroux, 2012), 10–11, 202 passim.

26. Huizinga, *Homo Ludens*, 1.

27. Huizinga, *Homo Ludens*, foreword, first page (pages not enumerated in foreword).

28. Huizinga, *Homo Ludens*, 46.

29. Huizinga, *Homo Ludens*, 13.

30. Huizinga, *Homo Ludens*, 28.

31. Huizinga, *Homo Ludens*, 1, 3, 9 passim.

32. Huizinga, *Homo Ludens*, 9. Because Huizinga is wary of reductionist and materialistic understandings of life, at times his rhetoric moves him to contrast too strongly the material and the biological with the mental or sacred. He does insist that animals play, and this is central to his explanation of why play is older than human cultures. In our time,

what is needed is an account of play that includes the material and biological in a more integrated way in an evolutionary context.

33. Huizinga, *Homo Ludens*, 8–14 passim.

34. The chapter by Randolph Feezell "A Pluralist Conception of Play," has been very illuminating with respect to the importance of the structure or form of games for understanding sports. I will further unpack Feezell's view that sports are most adequately understood as a kind of play in chapter 4. Randolph Feezell, "A Pluralist Conception of Play," in *The Philosophy of Play*, ed. Emily Ryall, Wendy Russell, and Malcolm MacLean (New York: Routledge, 2013).

35. Huizinga, *Homo Ludens*, 11.

36. Huizinga, *Homo Ludens*, 10, 18 passim.

37. Huizinga, *Homo Ludens*, 5.

38. Huizinga, *Homo Ludens*, 18–19.

39. Huizinga, *Homo Ludens*, 21 passim.

40. Huizinga, *Homo Ludens*, 21–22.

41. Robert N. Bellah, *Religion in Human Evolution: From the Paleolithic to the Axial Age* (Cambridge, MA: The Belknap Press of Harvard University Press, 2011), 92.

42. Bellah, *Religion in Human Evolution*, 92.

43. Romano Guardini, *The Spirit of the Liturgy*, trans. Ada Lane (New York: Crossroad, 1998), 62–63 passim.

44. Guardini, *Spirit of the Liturgy*, 63.

45. Guardini, *Spirit of the Liturgy*, 63 passim.

46. Guardini, *Spirit of the Liturgy*, 70, 71 passim.

47. Guardini, *Spirit of the Liturgy*, 71.

CHAPTER 2

1. William fitz Stephen, "Description of the City of London," in *English Historical Documents, 1042–1189*, ed. David C. Douglas and George W. Greenaway, vol. 2 (New York: Oxford University Press, 1953), 960.

2. Natalie Zemon Davis, *Society and Culture in Early Modern France* (Stanford, CA: Stanford University Press, 1975), 97–98.

3. Davis, *Society and Culture*, 98.

Notes

4. Huizinga, *Homo Ludens*, 21.

5. Victor Turner, "In and Out of Time: Festival, Liminality, and Communitas," *1978 Festival of American Folklife*, Smithsonian Institution, National Park Service (1978), 7.

6. Thomas Aquinas, *Summa Theologica* [ST], II–II, Q. 168, art. 4, trans. Fathers of the English Dominican Province (New York: Benziger Brothers, 1947); see also I–II, Q. 32, art. 1, obj. 3, 168–69. All quotations from the *Summa Theologica* are from this translation, unless otherwise noted.

7. Aquinas, ST II–II, Q. 168, art. 3, ad. 3. For an excellent discussion of Aquinas's approach to this topic set in its historical context, see Alasdair MacIntyre, "Natural Law as Subversive: The Case of Aquinas," *Journal of Medieval and Early Modern Studies* 26, no. 1 (1996): 61–83, esp. 55–57.

8. Aquinas, ST II–II, Q. 168, art. 2.

9. Aquinas, ST II–II, Q. 168, art. 4.

10. *Thomas Aquinas: Selected Writings*, ed. Ralph McInerny (New York: Penguin, 1998), 262. See *Summa Contra Gentiles* III, cap. 2; in the second case, the "end" Aquinas has in mind has to do with the effects of play on the human person. The end of games, he writes, is "mental relaxation, since after play we seem mentally keener and more studious" (*Thomas Aquinas Selected Writings*, 266). The end is not an extrinsic good unrelated to the activity itself, the way money or fame would be.

11. Aquinas, ST II–II, Q. 168, art. 2, ad. 3.

12. Aquinas, ST I–II, Q. 1, art. 6, ad. 1.

13. Aquinas, ST I–II, Q. 2, art. 6, ad. 1.

14. Aquinas, ST I–II, Q. 2, art. 6, ad. 1. He says in I–II, Q. 2, art. 6, ad. 3, "All desire delight in the same way as they desire good: and yet they desire delight by reason of the good, and not conversely."

15. While at play, he writes, "nothing further is sought than the soul's delight" (Aquinas, ST II–II, Q. 168, art. 2).

16. Aquinas, ST I–II, Q. 4, art. 1.

17. Josef Pieper, *Happiness and Contemplation*, trans. Richard and Clara Winston (New York: Pantheon, 1958), 49. Pieper translates the Latin *delectatio* as "joy," rather than "delight."

PLAY, SPORT, AND SPIRIT

18. Aquinas, ST I–II, Q. 1, art. 6, ad 2 passim. Regarding the question whether a person wills whatever he wills for his last end, God, Aquinas points out that whatever one desires, one does so "under the aspect of good." And if what he desires is not the perfect good, his last end, "he must, of necessity, desire it as tending to the perfect good, because the beginning of anything is always ordained to its completion; as is clearly the case in effects both of nature and of art" (ST I–II, Q. 1, art. 6).

19. Aquinas, ST I–II, Q. 1, art. 6, ad. 3 passim.

20. *Albert and Thomas: Selected Writings*, trans. and ed. Simon Tugwell (New York: Paulist Press, 1988), 527.

21. *Albert and Thomas: Selected Writings*, 527–28. By contemplation, Aquinas means different things at different times. In the first passage above, he seems to have in mind removing all distractions, including in our "interior house," and gathering ourselves and being fully present so that we can "play there." In the second passage, he is describing the "contemplation of wisdom," which has more of an intellectual component to it.

22. See Alessandra Rizzi, "Regulated Play at the End of the Middle Ages: The Work of Mendicant Preachers in Communal Italy," in *Sport and Culture in Early Modern Europe*, ed. John McClelland and Brian Merrilees (Toronto: Centre for Reformation and Renaissance Studies, 2010). Important theologians after Aquinas also reflected on play. In the fifteenth century, the humanist Cardinal Nicholas of Cusa wrote about the human and cultural significance of play and its relationship to the Christian life in his book *The Game of Spheres*. The setting for the book is that Nicholas has just returned from playing a new ball game with John and Albert, dukes of Bavaria, and he engages in dialogues with them about such topics as the creation of the world, the powers of the soul, the origin of various aspects of culture and the dynamics of the Christian life. For Nicholas, it is appropriate to make use of the ball game itself as the starting point for his reflection on these weighty topics for, as he puts it, "No honest game is entirely lacking in the capacity to instruct. I think that this delightful exercise with the ball represents a significant philosophy for us." Nicholas of Cusa, *De ludo globi* [*The Game of Spheres*], trans. Pauline Moffitt Watts (New York: Abaris Books, 1986), 55. Nicholas was an important reformer of the church

both in his native Germany and in Rome, where he lived in his later years at the invitation of his close friend Pope Pius II.

23. Aeneas Silvius Piccolomini, "The Education of Boys," in *Humanist Educational Treatises*, ed. and trans. Craig W. Kallendorf, The I Tatti Renaissance Library (Cambridge, MA: Harvard University Press, 2002), 143. In another context, Piccolomini writes that the young should "not be restrained too closely or they will become listless and lazy. They should be allowed to play and their pleasure should be indulged somewhat; this activity will summon forth their qualities of spirit and heart, they will come to distinguish good from bad, and will learn to detect the snares of the world and how to avoid them when they have gained maturity" (*Selected Letters of Aeneas Silvius Piccolomini*, ed. and trans. Albert R. Baca [Northridge, CA: San Fernando Valley State College, 1969], 20). Piccolomini (1405–64) was elected pope in 1458 and served as Pope Pius II until his death in 1464.

24. François de Dainville, *L'éducation des jésuites: XVI–XVIII siècles* (Paris: Éditions de Minuit, 1978). The information in these paragraphs is taken from de Dainville's account in this book.

25. *The Jesuit Ratio Studiorum of 1599*, trans. Allan P. Farrell (Washington, DC: Conference of Major Superiors of Jesuits, 1970).

26. The developments described in this paragraph were significant for education in general because the Jesuits were running some eight hundred schools in Europe and other parts of the world by 1773 when they were suppressed.

27. François Pierron, *Le bon precepteur ou La belle maniere de bien élever la jeunesse pour Dieu, & pour le beau monde* (Lyon: Chez Horace Boissat & G. Remeus, 1661), 218.

28. Pierron, *Le bon precepteur*, 218.

29. Joseph-François Lafitau, *Customs of the American Indians Compared with the Customs of Primitive Times*, vol. 2, ed. and trans. William N. Fenton and Elizabeth L. Moore (Toronto: Champlain Society, 1974), 189. This volume was first published in 1724. In addition to Thomas Aquinas's play ethic, another influence on the humanist and early Jesuit schools when it comes to play and sport were the classical sources of ancient Greece and Rome. The curriculum of the humanist and Jesuit schools centered around these writings and in them one could find examples of how physical and intellectual exercises went hand in

hand. Lafitau demonstrates remarkably detailed knowledge of the games of ancient Greece and Rome and discusses them at length in comparison with the Native American games. For further discussion, see Patrick Kelly, "The Earth is Shaking with Flying Feet," chap. 2 in *Catholic Perspectives on Sports: From Medieval to Modern Times* (Mahwah, NJ: Paulist Press, 2012).

30. *Journal of Paul du Ru, (February 1 to May 8, 1700), Missionary Priest to Louisiana*, trans. Ruth Lapham Butler (Chicago: The Caxton Club, 1934), 21, entry for February 27, 1700.

31. *Journal of Paul du Ru*. For a contrast between the attitudes of the Jesuits and other French Catholics toward Native American games and the attitudes of English Puritans toward them see George Eisen, "Early European Attitudes Toward Native American Sports and Pastimes," in *Ethnicity and Sport in North American History and Culture*, ed. George Eisen and David K. Wiggins (Westport, CT: Praeger Publishers, 1994).

32. "College of George-town, (Potomack) in the State of Maryland, United States of America, 1798," Washington, DC: Georgetown University, Lauinger Library, Georgetown University Archives [GUA].

33. "Georgetown College, In the District of Columbia, United States of America, under the Direction of the Incorporated Catholic Clergy of the State of Maryland," 1809, Georgetown University Archives [GUA].

34. Joseph T. Durkin, *Georgetown University: First in the Nation's Capital* (Garden City, NY: Doubleday, 1964), 12.

35. *Georgetown College Journal* 7, no. 2 (December 1878):15, [GUA].

36. *Georgetown College Journal*, 15.

37. *Georgetown College Journal*, 15.

38. *Georgetown College Journal*, 15.

39. The description of Dr. Nichols's visit to Notre Dame originally appeared in his book *Forty Years of American Life 1821–1861* (London: John Maxwell and Company, 1864; 2nd ed. New York: Stackpole Sons, 1937), 273–77, and is quoted by John Theodore Wack in his dissertation, "The University of Notre Dame du Lac: Foundations, 1842-1857," appendix 2, "A Description of Notre Dame du Lac in the 1850s," http://archives.nd.edu/research/texts/wack.htm.

Notes

40. Wack, "A Description of Notre Dame," passim.

41. T. A. C., "Celebration at Notre Dame University, Indiana," in *New York Tablet*, November 5, 1864, University of Notre Dame Archives; For other examples of Catholics at play in the nineteenth and twentieth centuries, see Patrick Kelly, "Ordinary People, Just Enjoying Themselves Like Human Beings," chap. 5 in *Catholic Perspectives on Sports: From Medieval to Modern Times* (New York: Paulist Press, 2012), 118–40; see also Patrick Kelly, "Catholics and Sports in the United States: An Alternative Tradition," in *U.S. Catholic Historian* 36, no. 2 (Spring 2018): 11–32.

42. Thomas C. Middleton, "Some Reminiscences. The Sports and Games in Vogue in Early Days at Villanova," in *History of Athletics: Villanova College* (Philadelphia: The Jenson Press, 1923), 7.

43. Middleton, "Some Reminiscences," 10.

44. Middleton, "Some Reminiscences," 12.

45. In this section, I am not attempting to describe all the different approaches of Protestants in the United States during this period. In the southern colonies, e.g., the valuing of leisure associated with aristocratic traditions in England continued. Regarding religious influences, this was made possible because there were more Anglicans in this region than in other regions. The Church of England broke from the Catholic Church in 1532 because Henry VIII wanted to divorce his wife, not over issues of theology or spirituality per se. And so, their spiritual descendants have always been closer to the Catholic Church with respect to religious culture, liturgy, and theology than Protestants who trace their origins to Martin Luther or John Calvin, and certainly than the Puritans. They were less critical of the playing of games and sport on feast days, for example. See Jane Carson, *Colonial Virginians at Play* (Williamsburg, VA: Colonial Williamsburg Foundation, 1989).

Neither am I attempting to describe all the other approaches to our topic in the United States during this period. Of course, many landowners in the southern states could enjoy leisure because of the scandalous institution of slavery. While Puritans and other white Protestants in the north were working very hard based on a particular ascetical and theological tradition, Africans who were enslaved were bought and sold as property and forced to work. One of the evil effects associated with this regime is that the cultural traditions in African countries of work, leisure, and recreation were interrupted. As a result, these cultural traditions were not able to influence the wider society in the United States during this period. Only recently have scholars begun to retrieve the experience of work of enslaved persons from their own perspective and to find in it a work ethic different from the well-studied "Protestant work ethic" of Max Weber. See Joan M. Martin, *More than Chains and Toil: A Christian Work Ethic of Enslaved Women* (Louisville, KY: Westminster John Knox Press, 2000). We will consider the approach of African American Christians to amusements, recreation, and play at the end of the nineteenth century later in this chapter.

Because of the tendency of Puritans and other Protestants in the early colonies to reject Native American cultural traditions completely, native traditional approaches to work, leisure, and play were also not able to influence the wider society. In the nineteenth century, government schools, often run by Protestant and Catholic missionaries, required the native children to abandon their cultural traditions and languages and to learn the culture of the Europeans and the English language. In the beginning of the twentieth century, Native American Jim Thorpe was too phenomenal an athlete to ignore. He may have been well known, but Native American cultural traditions in relation to work, leisure, and sport were not. It is only relatively recently that scholars are beginning to write about these native traditions. See Daniel McDonald and Leo McAvoy, "Native Americans and Leisure: State of the Research and Future Directions," *Journal of Leisure Research* 29, no. 2 (1997): 145–66; Karen Fox, "Leisure and Indigenous Peoples," *Leisure Studies* 25, no. 4 (October 2006): 403–9; Philip P. Arnold, *The Gift of Sports: Indigenous Ceremonial Dimensions of the Games We Love* (San Diego: Cognella, 2012); Temryss MacLean Lane, "North American Indigenous Soccer: Visibility, Intergenerational Healing, and Schelangen in Global Football" (master's thesis, UCLA, 2016), https://escholarship.org/uc/item/7kr2957k.

46. Washington Gladden, *Amusements: Their Uses and Abuses: A Sermon* (North Adams, MA: James T. Robinson, 1866), 6.

47. Gladden, *Amusements*, 7.

48. Gladden, *Amusements*, 5.

49. Edward Everett Hale, *Public Amusement for Poor and Rich: A Discourse* (Boston: Phillips, Sampson and Co., 1857), 21.

50. Hale, *Public Amusement for Poor and Rich*, 5.

51. Horace Bushnell, *Christian Nurture* (Eugene, OR: Wipf and Stock, 2000, first published in 1847), 17.

52. Bushnell, *Christian Nurture*, 339–40.

53. Bushnell, *Christian Nurture*, 342.

54. Bushnell, *Christian Nurture*, 343.

55. *W. E. B. Du Bois on Sociology and the Black Community*, ed. Dan S. Green and Edwin D. Driver (Chicago: University of Chicago Press, 1978), 228 passim.

56. Du Bois, *On Sociology and the Black Community*, 231, 232.

57. Du Bois, *On Sociology and the Black Community*, 231.

58. Du Bois, *On Sociology and the Black Community*, 235.

59. Du Bois, *On Sociology and the Black Community*, 230, 231 passim.

60. Tony Ladd and James A. Mathisen, *Muscular Christianity: Evangelical Protestants and the Development of American Sport* (Grand Rapids, MI: Baker Books, 1999); Clifford Wallace Putney, *Muscular Christianity: The Strenuous Mood in American Protestantism, 1880–1920* (Cambridge, MA: Harvard University Press, 2001).

CHAPTER THREE

1. John Henry Newman, *The Idea of a University* (Garden City, NY: Image Books, 1959) originally published in 1852; Josef Pieper, *Leisure, the Basis of Culture* (South Bend, IN: St. Augustine's Press, 1998); Josef Pieper, *Happiness and Contemplation*, trans. Richard and Clara Winston (London: Faber and Faber, 1959), see pp. 50–51 and 71–72; Walter Kerr, *The Decline of Pleasure* (New York: Simon and Schuster, 1962).

2. Newman, *Idea of a University*, 134.

3. Newman, *Idea of a University*, 130, 147 passim.

4. Hugo Rahner, *Man at Play*, trans. Brian Battershaw and Edward Quinn (New York: Herder and Herder, 1967), 19, 24.

5. Rahner, *Man at Play*, 24.

6. Paul Quenon, *In Praise of the Useless Life: A Monk's Memoir* (Notre Dame, IN: Ave Maria Press, 2018), 5; Jonathan Malesic writes about how time he spent in a monastery helped him to tame the demon of the "ceaseless, obsessive American work ethic" in "Taming the Demon:

How Desert Monks Put Work in its Place," *Commonweal* 146, no. 3 (February 8, 2019).

    7. Quenon, *In Praise of the Useless Life*, 5 passim.

    8. A. Bartlett Giamatti, *Take Time for Paradise: Americans and Their Games* (New York: Summit Books, 1991), 28 passim.

    9. Michael Novak, *The Joy of Sports: Endzones, Bases, Baskets, Balls, and the Consecration of the American Spirit* (Lanham, MD: Madison Books, 1967, 1988, 1994), 226–27, 228 passim.

    10. Novak, *Joy of Sports*, 227.

    11. Novak, *Joy of Sports*, 224, 225–26, 227 passim.

    12. R. Worth Frank, "Protestantism and Play," *Social Progress* 26 (1935): 5.

    13. Peter Berger, *A Rumor of Angels: Modern Society and the Rediscovery of the Supernatural* (Garden City, NY: Doubleday, 1969), 58–60 passim.

    14. Berger, *Rumor of Angels*, 60.

    15. Harvey Cox, *The Feast of Fools: A Theological Essay on Festivity and Fantasy* (Cambridge, MA: Harvard University Press, 1969), 146.

    16. Cox, *Feast of Fools*, 13.

    17. Jurgen Moltmann, *Theology of Play* (New York: Harper & Row, 1972), 19.

    18. Moltmann, *Theology of Play*, 19.

    19. Moltmann, *Theology of Play*, quoted on p. 20.

    20. Moltmann, *Theology of Play*, 21.

    21. It is true that some Protestant students attended Catholic colleges in the nineteenth and early twentieth centuries. They would have been exposed in these schools to the holistic approach to education and the kinds of games and sports described in the last chapter. But they were relatively few. They also would have faced significant challenges in trying to import the approach to play and sport they experienced in these schools into the wider society, given the mainstream cultural, economic, and theological trends which exalted work and were suspicious of play.

    22. Charles Taylor, *A Secular Age* (Cambridge, MA: Belknap Press of Harvard University, 2007), 498.

    23. Taylor, *Secular Age*, 771.

    24. "The Church," *Papal Teachings* (Boston: Daughters of St. Paul, 1960), 22.

Notes

25. Taylor, *Secular Age*, 771.

26. *Joy of Sports*, xiv. He does have a profile of Holy Cross priest Robert Griffin, chaplain to the Notre Dame football team. But even here the focus is on the conversion of Fr. Griffin to believing in the power and goodness of football (35–39).

27. See "Pope Pius IX: Syllabus of Errors, 8 December 1864," in *Readings in Church History*, ed. Colman J. Barry (Westminster, MD: Christian Classics, 1985), 992–95; and "Encyclical, 'Pascendi Dominici Gregis,' Condemning the Doctrines of Modernism, 8 September 1907," in *Readings in Church History*, 1030–37. For the condemnations of Americanism, see specifically the "Apostolical Letter *Testem Benevolentiae*, January 22, 1899, addressed to His Eminence Cardinal Gibbons, Archbishop of Baltimore," in *The Great Encyclical Letters of Pope Leo XIII* (New York: Benziger Brothers, 1903), 441–53.

28. Pedro Arrupe, "Letter on Inculturation, to the Whole Society," in *Other Apostolates Today* (St. Louis: Institute of Jesuit Sources, 1978), 179.

29. See, e.g., Steven J. Overman, *The Influence of the Protestant Ethic on Sport and Recreation* (Brookfield, VT: Avebury, 1997); Clifford Wallace Putney, *Muscular Christianity: Manhood and Sports in Protestant America, 1880–1920* (Cambridge, MA: Harvard University Press, 2001); Dennis Brailsford, "Religion and Sport in Eighteenth-Century England: 'For the Encouragement of Piety and Virtue, and for the Preventing or Punishing of Vice, Profaneness and Immorality,'" in *British Journal of Sports History* 1, no. 2 (September 1984): 166–83; James A. Mathisen, "From Muscular Christians to Jocks for Jesus," in *Christian Century* (January 1–8, 1992); Joachim K. Ruhl, "Religion and Amusements in Sixteenth-and Seventeenth-Century England: 'Time might be better bestowed, and besides wee see sin acted,'" in *British Journal of Sports History* 1, no. 2 (1984): 125–65; Nancy Struna, "Puritans and Sports: The Irretrievable Tide of Change," in *Journal of Sport History* 4 (Spring 1977): 1–21; Tony Ladd and James A. Mathisen, *Muscular Christianity: Evangelical Protestants and the Development of American Sport* (Grand Rapids, MI: Baker Books, 1999).

30. See *Sport and Religion*, ed. Shirl J. Hoffman (Champaign, IL: Human Kinetics Books, 1992), esp. 1–61; *Religion and Sport: The Meeting of Sacred and Profane*, Charles S. Prebish (Westport, CT: Greenwood

Press, 1993); *From Season to Season: Sports as American Religion*, ed. Joseph L. Price (Macon, GA: Mercer University Press, 2001).

31. *Influence of the Protestant Ethic*, 194.

32. See Brian W. W. Aitken, "The Emergence of Born Again Sport," in Prebish, *Religion and Sport*.

33. See, e.g., for Catholics: Patrick Kelly, *Catholic Perspectives on Sports: From Medieval to Modern Times* (Mahwah, NJ: Paulist Press, 2012); Patrick Kelly, "Catholics and Sports in the United States: An Alternative Tradition," *U.S. Catholic Historian* 36, no. 2 (Spring 2018): 11–32; Richard R. Gaillardetz, "For the Love of the Game," in *Youth Sport and Spirituality: Catholic Perspectives*, ed. Patrick Kelly (Notre Dame, IN: University of Notre Dame Press, 2015); Kristin Komyatte Sheehan, "Playing Like a Champion Today II: Youth Sport and Growth in Body, Mind and Spirit," in Kelly, *Youth Sport and Spirituality*; F. Clark Power and Lillie K. Rodgers, "From Play to Virtue: The Social, Moral, and Religious Dimensions of Youth Sport," *Journal of Religion and Society*, Supplement 20 Special Issue: "Catholics and Sport in a Global Context," ed. Patrick Kelly (2019): 23–44; Mark Nesti, "Persons First, Athletes Second: If Aquinas Came to the English Premier League" *Journal of Religion and Society*, Supplement 20 Special Issue (2019): 94–105. For Protestants see: Robert K. Johnston, *The Christian at Play* (Eugene, OR: Wipf and Stock, 1997); Doug Hochstetler, Peter Hopsicker, and Scott Kretchmar, "Created to Play: Thoughts on Play, Sport, and the Christian Life," in *The Image of God in the Human Body: Essays on Christianity and Sports*, ed. Donald L. Deardorff and John White (Lewiston, NY: Edwin Mellen Press, 2008); Mark Hamilton, "Sport as Spectacle and the Perversion of Pla," in Deardorff and White, *Image of God in the Human Body*; Gregg Twietmeyer, "Religion, Theology and Sport," in *Routledge Handbook of the Philosophy of Sport*, ed. Mike McNamee and William J. Morgan (New York: Routledge, 2015).

34. Matt Hoven, Andrew Parker, and Nick J. Watson, eds., *Sport and Christianity: Practices for the Twenty-First Century* (London: T & T Clark, 2020), xvii.

35. Hoven, Parker, and Watson, *Sport and Christianity*, 169.

Notes

36. Lincoln Harvey, *A Brief Theology of Sport* (Eugene, OR: Cascade Books, 2014), 83, 84, 89 passim.

37. Harvey, *Brief Theology of Sport*, 96. In an earlier chapter on medieval Catholicism and sport, he fails to mention Thomas Aquinas.

38. Robert Johnston, "How Might Theology of Play Inform Theology of Sport?" in Hoven, Parker, and Watson, *Sport and Christianity*, 15, 16 passim.

39. Robert Johnston, "How Might Theology of Play Inform Theology of Sport?", 16.

40. Contemporary philosophers have been reflecting on the relationship between play and sport longer than theologians have. As was mentioned, in chap. 4 I will be making use of the reflections of Randolph Feezell in this regard. See, e.g., Bernard Suits, "Words on Play," *Journal of the Philosophy of Sport* 4, no. 1 (1977): 117–31; Bernard Suits, "The Elements of Sport," in *Philosophic Inquiry in Sport*, ed. Klaus V. Meier and William J. Morgan (Champaign, IL: Human Kinetics, 1988, 1995); Bernard Suits, "Tricky Triad: Games, Play and Sport," in Meier and Morgan, *Philosophic Inquiry in Sport*; Klaus Meier, "Triad Trickery: Playing With Sport and Games," in Meier and Morgan, *Philosophic Inquiry in Sport*; Klaus V. Meier, "An Affair of Flutes: An Appreciation of Play," in Meier and Morgan, *Philosophic Inquiry in Sport*; Drew A. Hyland, "'And That Is the Best Part of Us': Human Being and Play," *Journal of the Philosophy of Sport* 4, no. 1 (1977): 36–49; Lynne Belaief, "Meanings of the Body," *Journal of the Philosophy of Sport* 4, no. 1 (1977): 50–67; Robert G. Osterhoudt, ed., published under the auspices of Philosophic Society for the Study of Sport; William J. Morgan, "Play, Utopia, and Dystopia: Prologue to a Ludic Theory of the State," *Journal of the Philosophy of Sport* 9, no. 1 (1982): 30–42; Daniel Dombrowski, *Contemporary Athletics and Ancient Greek Ideals* (Chicago, IL: The University of Chicago Press, 2009); Heather L. Reid, *Introduction to the Philosophy of Sport* (Lanham, MD: Rowman and Littlefield, 2012), see esp. chap. 3, "Sport and Play," and chap. 4, "Sport and Games." Randolph Feezell, *Sport, Play and Ethical Reflection* (Urbana: University of Illinois Press, 2004); Randolph Feezell, "A Pluralist Conception of

Play," in *Philosophy of Play*, ed. Emily Ryall, Wendy Russell, and Malcolm MacLean (New York: Routledge, 2013).

CHAPTER FOUR

1. Gordon M. Burghardt, *The Genesis of Animal Play: Testing the Limits* (Cambridge, MA: Massachusetts Institute of Technology, 2005), xiv.

2. Sergio M. Pellis, Gordon M. Burghardt, Elisabetta Palagi, and Marc Mangel, "Modeling Play: Distinguishing between Origins and Current Functions," *Adaptive Behavior* 23, no. 6 (December 2015): 331–39; at 331.

3. Burghardt, *Genesis of Animal Play*, xiii. As we read in the first chapter, Romano Guardini expressed a similar concern as these authors when he pointed out that if we consider phenomena only with respect to their "purpose," we will not always understand them adequately.

4. Burghardt, *Genesis of Animal Play*, see 70–82.

5. Burghardt, *Genesis of Animal Play*, 81.

6. Burghardt, *Genesis of Animal Play*, 119.

7. Pellis, Burghardt, Palagi, and Mangel, "Modeling Play."

8. Gordon M. Burghardt, "A Brief Glimpse at the Long Evolutionary History of Play," *Animal Behavior and Cognition* 1, no. 2 (May 2014): 94.

9. Burghardt, "A Brief Glimpse," 92.

10. Burghardt, *Genesis of Animal Play*, see chart on 120.

11. Gordon M. Burghardt, "On the Origins of Play," in *Play in Animals and Humans*, ed. Peter K. Smith (New York: Basil Blackwell, 1984), 34. There are gradations in terms of whether an animal is precocial or altricial. And there are exceptions to the general rule here. My colleague Amy Bauer pointed out that horses and guinea pigs are more precocial than other mammals, for example. "Yet horses definitely play, as can guinea pigs" (email message to author).

12. Burghardt, "On the Origins of Play," 34.

13. Burghardt, *Genesis of Animal Play*, 172.

14. Burghardt, "A Brief Glimpse," 92 passim. Burghardt refers to the research of H. Pontzer, et al., "Primate Energy Expenditure and Life

Notes

History," *Proceedings of the National Academy of Sciences of the United States of America* 111, no. 4 (January 13, 2014): 1433–37.

15. Burghardt, "A Brief Glimpse," 92.

16. Burghardt, *Genesis of Animal Play*, 121.

17. Burghardt, *Genesis of Animal Play*, 121. Italics in original. Robert Bellah makes use of Alfred Shutz's notion of multiple realities to understand the significance of play. In human societies daily life is the workaday world where we must do many things to survive, what he calls life "online." It is the "wide awake," grown-up world, practical and pragmatic, governed by the means-ends schema, and it takes place in standard time and space. But this world is culturally and symbolically constructed, not the world "as it actually is." We can also experience life "offline" when we don't need to make our way in the world and the pressure to survive is off. For Bellah, "the capacity to go offline in a number of ways, which is present even in simple organisms but much more extensive in complex ones and especially so among humans, may be one of our greatest capacities of all, and...religion, along with science and art, may be the result of that capacity to go offline." (Robert Bellah, *Religion in Human Evolution: From the Paleolithic to the Axial Age* [Cambridge, MA: The Belknap Press of Harvard University Press, 2011], xxii.)

18. Because the interview took place before he became Pope Benedict XVI, I will refer to him in this section as Cardinal Ratzinger. The interview was originally published in German in *Ordinariats-Korrespondenz*, 1978. Archdiocese of Munich-Freising Bulletin (03–15/78); he later included the interview in J. K. Ratzinger, *Suchen, was droben ist. Meditationen das Jahrhindurch* (Freiburg im Breisgau: Herder, 1985), 107–11; and did the same when he was Pope Benedict XVI in *Das Werk: Bibliographisches Hilfsmittel zur Erschließung des literarisch-theologischen Werkes von Joseph Ratzinger bis zur Papstwahl* (Augsburg: Sankt Ulrich, 2009). The English translation is by Teresa Benedetta, "In His Own Words: Texts and Interviews before JR Became Pope," https://www.freeforumzone.com/mobile/d/354533.

19. Benedetta, "In His Own Words."

20. Benedetta, "In His Own Words." I have taken the liberty to translate the German word *Zweck* as "purpose" here, rather than goal. Benedetta translates the term as goal, but this can be confusing or even

misleading in the context of discussing sports, which clearly have "goals."

21. Benedetta, "In His Own Words," passim.

22. Benedetta, "In His Own Words."

23. Benedetta, "In His Own Words." Although he was writing before Burghardt's research on the genesis of animal play, Lutheran theologian Wolfgang Pannenberg's reflections on play help us to understand the relationship between themes in Burghardt's research and Cardinal Ratzinger's reflections: "Through play, human beings develop their capacities for behavior that is not goal directed but can secondarily be used for any goal chosen. In this sense, play is, first of all, the 'beginning of freedom.'" Pannenberg emphasizes the greater freedom from 'instinct" human beings have when compared with other animals. However, he writes, "This release from the ties of instinct is, of course, only one side of freedom. Freedom reaches completion only when individuals impose ties on themselves that are interwoven with their social relations. This side of freedom, too, is developed through play." Wolfgang Pannenberg, "Foundations of Culture," in *Anthropology in Theological Perspective*, trans. Matthew J. O'Connor (Edinburgh: T & T Clark, 1985), 323.

24. Benedetta, "In His Own Words."

25. Benedetta, "In His Own Words." Earlier in the interview, Ratzinger referred to the freedom of play as a kind of foretaste of a future paradise. Here he refers to sport as a stepping over from daily life in the direction of "our lost paradise," which for him would mean human existence before original sin in the garden of Eden. But it is possible to understand these images as related within his way of framing things. For the Fathers of the Church, sin in all its manifestations defaces the image and likeness of God in which we were created. And redemption had to do with recovering this image and likeness of God in ourselves. From this perspective, the recovery of the image and likeness of God associated with our beginning in the garden of Eden is also related to our future glory or being part of the paradise of heaven. For a different way of understanding original sin in an evolutionary context, see Stephen J. Duffy, "Our Hearts of Darkness: Original Sin Revisited," *Theological Studies* 49, no. 4 (1988): 597–622.

Notes

CHAPTER FIVE

1. Randolph Feezell, *Sport, Play, and Ethical Reflection* (Urbana and Chicago: University of Illinois, 2004), 28.

2. Randolph Feezell, "A Pluralist Conception of Play," in *The Philosophy of Play*, ed. Emily Ryall, Wendy Russell, and Malcolm MacLean (New York: Routledge, 2013).

3. Feezell cites Robin Marantz Henig in this regard, "Taking Play Seriously," *New York Times Magazine*, February 17, 2008.

4. Feezell, "A Pluralist Conception," 16.

5. Feezell, "A Pluralist Conception," 18.

6. Fred Feldman, *Pleasure and the Good Life: Concerning the Nature, Varieties and Plausibility of Hedonism* (Oxford: Clarendon Press, 2004), 56.

7. Quoted in Feezell, "A Pluralist Conception," 22. Suits offers a pithier rendering of this definition as well: "Playing a game is the voluntary attempt to overcome unnecessary obstacles." (Suits, quoted in Feezell, "A Pluralist Conception," 22.)

8. See Feezell, "A Pluralist Conception," 23.

9. Gadamer, quoted in Feezell, "A Pluralist Conception," 25, 26 passim.

10. Feezell, "A Pluralist Conception," 28 passim.

11. Feezell, "A Pluralist Conception," 28, 29 passim.

12. Feezell, "A Pluralist Conception," 27–28.

13. Feezell, "A Pluralist Conception," 29.

14. Of course, it also happened on occasion that I didn't want to go to practice, and then once I was there, I didn't identify with what was going on, did not particularly want to engage in it, and did not enjoy it. If this happened too often, I would likely have become discouraged and lost interest in the sport.

15. Frithjof Bergmann, *On Being Free* (Notre Dame, IN: University of Notre Dame Press, 1977), 64.

16. Bergmann, *On Being Free*, 71.

17. Bergmann, *On Being Free*, 72

18. Bergmann, *On Being Free*, 72. See also in this respect Victor Frankl, *Man's Search for Meaning: An Introduction to Logotherapy* (New York: Simon and Schuster, 1984).

19. Bergmann, *On Being Free*, 37.
20. Bergmann, *On Being Free*, 92.
21. Bergmann, *On Being Free*, 93.
22. Bergmann, *On Being Free*, 92. Bergmann uses metaphors associated with movement to describe the experience of freedom, such as "free flow," "natural flow," and "spontaneous flow," which highlight its dynamic character (92 and 93). It also feels natural and effortless, because we are simply being ourselves and giving expression to that in the world.

23. Bergmann, *On Being Free*, 93. According to Bergmann, artists and intellectuals have a special relation to freedom understood in this way, given that it is "an indispensable necessity for their everyday work.... Their writing either suits themselves, and is quite stringently a self-expression, which regardless of the arduous work it may require, nonetheless in some sense naturally flows from them, or it simply cannot be done at all.... The process through which an artist finds his own style or his own 'voice' could thus be a symbol for much of what we have tried to say" (ibid.).

24. Bergmann, *On Being Free*, 97.
25. Bergmann, *On Being Free*, 100.
26. Bergmann, *On Being Free*, 100–101.
27. Randolph Feezell, *Sport, Play, and Ethical Reflection* (Urbana: University of Illinois Press, 2004), 22.
28. See Jay Coakley, "Sport Specialization and its Effects," in *Learning Culture Through Sports: Perspectives on Society and Organized Sports*, eds. Lampman and Spickard, 2nd ed. (Lanham, MD: Rowman & Littlefield Publishers, 2011).
29. Coakley, "Sport Specialization," 14 passim.
30. Hans-Georg Gadamer, *Truth and Method*, trans. and rev. Joel Weinsheimer and Donald G. Marshall (London: Bloomsbury, 2004), 112.
31. Feezell, *Sport, Play, and Ethical Reflection*, 28, 29 passim.
32. Feezell, *Sport, Play, and Ethical Reflection*, 25.
33. Feezell, *Sport, Play, and Ethical Reflection*, 25–26. Italics in original.
34. John Cottingham, Robert Stoothoff, and Dugald Murdoch, *The Philosophical Writings of Descartes: Volume 1* (Cambridge: Cambridge University Press, 2012) at VI 32: CSM I 127. As we entered the modern world, the human "spirit," which according to St. Paul makes the

Notes

human being capable of relationship with the Holy Spirit, tended to be omitted from descriptions of the human person.

35. Maurice Merleau-Ponty, *The Phenomenology of Perception*, trans. Colin Smith (London: Routledge and Kegan Paul, 1962), 235.

36. Klaus V. Meier, "Affair of Flutes: An Appreciation of Play," in *Philosophic Inquiry in Sport*, ed. William J. Morgan and Klaus V. Meier (Champaign, IL: Human Kinetics, 1995), 125.

37. Klaus V. Meier, "Embodiment, Sport, and Meaning," in Morgan and Meier, *Philosophic Inquiry in Sport*, 94; for a discussion of how embodied action precedes cognition and perception, see also chap. 3 of Hans Joas, *Creativity of Action* (Chicago: University of Chicago Press, 1996).

38. Margaret Farley, *Just Love: A Framework for Christian Sexual Ethics* (New York: Continuum, 2006), 129. According to Farley, this approach is grounded in basic Christian doctrines. As she puts it: "At the heart of Christian belief is the affirmation that not only is the human body good, but it is intrinsic to being human. Created by God, sustained in being by God, offered an unlimited future by the promises of God in Jesus Christ, each human person—embodied and inspirited—has the possibility of and the call to a destiny of relation and wholeness as embodied spirit, inspirited body" (ibid., 131).

39. Pope Benedict XVI, "To Representatives of the Italian Ski Instructors," November 15, 2010.

40. Bergmann, *On Being Free*, 60.

41. Christ is the model in this regard, who according to St. Paul "was not 'Yes and No'; but in him it is always 'Yes'" (2 Cor 1:19). Indeed, St. Paul sees Christ himself as the "Yes" of God's promises. "For in him every one of God's promises is a 'Yes'" (2 Cor 1: 20).

42. Ignatius of Loyola, *The Spiritual Exercises and Selected Works*, ed. George E. Ganss (New York: Paulist Press, 1991), 201.

43. Jules J. Toner, *A Commentary on St. Ignatius' Rules for the Discernment of Spirits* (St. Louis: The Institute of Jesuit Sources, 1982), 86.

44. "Autograph Directory of St. Ignatius," in *On Giving the Spiritual Exercises: The Early Jesuit Manuscript Directories and the Official Directory of 1599*, trans. and ed. Martin E. Palmer (St. Louis: The Institute of Jesuit Sources, 1996), 8–9. In his spiritual diary, Ignatius uses words such as *quiet, gentle, warm, sweet*, and *delightful* to describe spiritual consolation. (See, e.g., pp. 82–85 in *St. Ignatius of Loyola: Personal*

Writings, trans. with Introduction and Notes by Joseph A. Munitiz and Philip Endean (New York: Penguin Books, 1996)].

45. Loyola, *Spiritual Exercises*, 202. I am following Jules Toner's approach to understanding spiritual consolation, which starts with what the term means in ordinary usage: Toner, *A Commentary on St. Ignatius' Rules*, 84–89, 286–92; see also Brian O. McDermott, "Spiritual Consolation and Its Role in the Second Time of Election," *Studies in the Spirituality of Jesuits* 50, no. 4 (Winter 2018). According to Michael Buckley, SJ, it is not necessary to consider the broader meaning of the term *consolation* to understand Ignatius's spiritual consolation. For him, any affective experience, whether pleasant or not, that leads a person to God can be considered spiritual consolation (Michael J. Buckley, "The Structure of the Rules for Discernment of Spirits," *The Way Supplement* 20 [Autumn 1973]: 19–37). Toner gives his reasons for disagreeing with Buckley's approach in Toner, *A Commentary*, 286–92; McDermott offers a critique of Buckley's approach in McDermott, "Spiritual Consolation and Its Role," 19–21, 26. For Ignatius, there is also consolation which is deceptive, which can lead people who are further along in the Christian life astray. Such persons can no longer be tempted to things that are obviously sinful, so they are led astray by experiences of consolation or by "good and holy thoughts" that over time divert them or lead to something immoral, or to disturbance and disquiet, loss of peace and tranquility. (See Loyola, *Spiritual Exercises*, 205–7.) In this chapter I am only treating genuine spiritual consolation.

46. Loyola, *Spiritual Exercises*, 201. Ignatius also says in this rule—before he describes spiritual consolation and desolation—that it is "characteristic of the good spirit to stir up courage and strength, consolations, tears, inspirations and tranquility." Toner points out that the courage and strength mentioned here is not to be understood as tied explicitly to spiritual consolation. God gives this at all times, including during spiritual desolation (about which more later). (Jules J. Toner, *A Commentary*, 68–69.)

47. Loyola, *Spiritual Exercises*, 207 passim. For Ignatius, our thoughts, acts of the will, or affective experiences come from one of three sources: from ourselves under some control of our free will, from a good spirit (God or an angel), or from an evil spirit.

Notes

48. Dean Brackley, *The Call to Discernment in Troubled Times: New Perspectives on the Transformative Wisdom of Ignatius of Loyola* (New York: Crossroad, 2004), 57. It is important to point out that spiritual consolation is not to be equated with a superficial kind of happiness, associated with things going well in our day, or having a life of ease or pleasure. For Ignatius we can experience spiritual consolation when we experience sorrow for our sins or in relation to the sufferings of Christ. The process of reconciliation between two people is usually difficult and painful, but as the relationship is repaired and forgiveness is experienced, the persons may experience a deep peace and a sense of God's presence. Sometimes family members during a funeral for a loved one can experience a kind of peace and tranquility associated with God's comforting presence. In our time, we may experience such consolation as we let our hearts be moved by the suffering of oppressed or marginalized people in the world.

49. Of course, it is also possible that there are parts of a person who is fundamentally progressing from good to better that are egoistic or resistant to the movement of the Spirit. When the Holy Spirit touches these parts of the person, the experience will be unsettling and disturbing, rather than congruent, consoling, and effortless.

50. William A. Barry, *Spiritual Direction and the Encounter with God: A Theological Inquiry*, rev. ed. (Mahwah, NJ: Paulist Press, 2004), 78.

51. Barry, *Spiritual Direction and the Encounter with God*, 78. Barry writes these words in the context of discussing discernment and spiritual consolation. And having a sense of the rightness of a way of life, happiness and fulfillment are characteristic of consolation. The context of faith and living out God's will also suggests that he is referring to an experience of spiritual consolation. However, "attunement to the one action of God" or "collaborating with God who is laboring" take place at a level of one's being that is deeper than the experience of spiritual consolation and may be occurring at times when one is not experiencing spiritual consolation.

52. Toner, *A Commentary*, 124–25.

53. Loyola, *Spiritual Exercises*, 202–4; see also "Autograph Directory of St. Ignatius," in *On Giving the Spiritual Exercises: The Early Jesuit Manuscript Directories and the Official Directory of 1599*, trans. and ed. Martin E. Palmer (St. Louis: The Institute of Jesuit Sources, 1996), 8–9.

54. Loyola, *Spiritual Exercises*, 207. Ignatius's advice for handling spiritual desolation is to be patient and remember that consolation will return. It is important to be gentle with ourselves at such times. But it is also important to stay faithful to prayer and our spiritual practices, given that we can be tempted to give up on them out of discouragement during such times. While experiences of desolation can be painful, during these times God can also bring healing and new life.

55. Patrick M. Kelly, "Loved into Freedom and Service: Lay Experiences of the Exercises in Daily Life," *Studies in the Spirituality of Jesuits* 39, no. 2 (Summer 2007): 30–31. Michael is a pseudonym for one of twenty-two lay people I interviewed about their experience of the Spiritual Exercises retreat made over the course of nine months for this article. Spiritual desolation is not always a sign that a person is moving in the wrong direction with a decision. It could be that there is a part of the person that is egoistic or resistant to what the Spirit is inviting him or her to do. And the desolation is arising from that part of the person. In such a case, the grace to pray for would be interior freedom.

56. Kelly, "Loved into Freedom," 31.

57. Kelly, "Loved into Freedom," 31.

58. Bergmann, *On Being Free*, 97. The experience of spiritual desolation is not necessarily or always associated with a lack of freedom either in Bergmann's sense or in Ignatius's sense of interior freedom. Our freedom operates at a different level of our being than spiritual consolation and desolation.

59. Bergmann, *On Being Free*, 97. In the Christian tradition and for Ignatius, the true self would be understood as the person created in the image and likeness of God. This topic will be discussed in the next section.

60. Loyola, *Spiritual Exercises*, 336.

61. Loyola, *Spiritual Exercises*, 162–65.

62. Thomas Merton, *The Silent Life* (New York: Farrar, Straus & Giroux, 1957), 22. Thomas Merton was significantly influenced by the medieval Franciscan philosopher Duns Scotus. For Scotus, and in the Franciscan tradition more broadly, it is primarily in our freedom that we are created in the image and likeness of God. As Kenan Osborne, OFM, put it: "We have free will, and it is particularly in this free will that we evidence the image of God." "Incarnation, Individuality and Diversity:

Notes

How Does Christ Reveal the Unique Value of Each Person and Thing?" *The Cord: A Franciscan Spiritual Review* 45, no. 3 (May–June 1995). Scotus's emphasis on God creating each thing and person in its individuality and particularity (what he called "haecceity") also influenced Merton's writings on the true self. See Daniel P. Horan, *The Franciscan Heart of Thomas Merton: A New Look at the Spiritual Inspiration of his Life, Thought, and Writing* (Notre Dame, IN: Ave Maria, 2014).

63. Bernard of Clairvaux, *Selected Works*, trans. G. R. Evans (New York: Paulist Press, 1987), 83. The value of Merton's approach and that of the Church Fathers is that they are pointing to a reality in human experience that is deeper, truer than sin or even its effects. In this sense, when we sin, we are not only offending God, and perhaps hurting others, but are also not being true to ourselves. On the other hand, as I mentioned in the last chapter, some contemporary theologians are questioning in light of an evolutionary understanding of the world the validity of the view that there was a time of innocence before a fall. For a different way of understanding original sin in an evolutionary context, see Stephen J. Duffy, "Our Hearts of Darkness: Original Sin Revisited," *Theological Studies* 49 (1988): 597–622.

64. Thomas Merton, *New Seeds of Contemplation* (New York: New Directions, 1972), 30.

65. Merton, *New Seeds*, 31.

66. Merton, *New Seeds*, 31–32.

67. Merton, *New Seeds*, 32. Italics in source.

68. Thomas Merton, *No Man is an Island* (New York: Harcourt Brace, 1955), 132.

69. Quoted in Quenon, *In Praise of the Useless Life*, 4.

70. Merton, *New Seeds*, 31.

71. *Gerard Manley Hopkins: Selected Poetry*, ed. Catherine Phillips (Oxford: Oxford University Press, 2009), 129.

72. *Gerard Manley Hopkins: Selected Poetry*, 115.

73. Robert Inchausti, ed., *Echoing Silence: Thomas Merton on the Vocation of Writing* (Boston: New Seeds, 2007), 198–9. Merton wrote this letter on June 11, 1963.

74. Walter Ong, preface to Hugo Rahner, *Man at Play*, trans. Brian Battershaw and Edward Quinn (New York: Herder and Herder, 1967), x.

75. Ong, preface to Rahner, *Man at Play*, xi.
76. Ong, preface to Rahner, *Man at Play*, xiii.
77. Ong, preface to Rahner, *Man at Play*, xiv.
78. Ong, preface to Rahner, *Man at Play*, xiv.

CHAPTER SIX

1. *Beyond Boredom and Anxiety: The Experience of Play in Work and Games* (San Francisco: Jossey-Bass, 1975), xi.
2. Johan Huizinga, *Homo Ludens: A Study of the Play Element in Culture* (Boston: Beacon Press, 1950), 2.
3. Mihaly Csikszentmihalyi, "Play and Intrinsic Rewards," *The Journal of Humanistic Psychology* 15, no. 3 (Summer 1975): 42; D. W. Winnicott makes the same critique of Melanie Klein, for whom focus on play was only in its usefulness, *Playing and Reality* (New York: Routledge Classics, 2005), 53.
4. Csikszentmihalyi, "Play and Intrinsic Rewards," xii.
5. Csikszentmihalyi, "Play and Intrinsic Rewards," 48.
6. As mentioned earlier, this dichotomy between play and work, which is something many people in the United States take for granted today, has more to do with the Puritan work ethic and industrialization, which have shaped our sensibility in such important ways, than with "the way things are." Related to this topic see, e.g., Keith Thomas, "Work and Leisure in Pre-Industrial Society," in *Past and Present* 29, no. 1 (December 1964): 50–66, and Victor Turner, "Liminal to Liminoid, in Play, Flow, and Ritual: An Essay in Comparative Symbology," *Rice University Studies* 60, no. 3 (Summer 1974).
7. Mihaly Csikszentmihalyi, *Beyond Boredom and Anxiety: The Experience of Play in Work and Games* (San Francisco: Jossey-Bass, 1975), 185.
8. Csikszentmihalyi, *Beyond Boredom*, 37.
9. Csikszentmihalyi, *Beyond Boredom*, 37. In 1996, Csikszentmihalyi wrote an important book titled *Creativity: Flow and the Psychology of Discovery and Invention* (New York: Harper Collins, 1996) in which he further explored the phenomenology of creativity in relation to flow theory. Regarding flow and religious experiences, see Mihaly

Notes

Csikszentmihalyi, "Flow Experience," in *The Encyclopedia of Religion*, ed. Mircea Eliade, vol. 5 (New York: Macmillan, 1987), 361–63.

10. According to Csikszentmihalyi, the discipline of psychology was led by reductionist accounts of human existence, the extensive influence of the natural sciences, and the medical approach to mental illness to a "mechanistic orientation which often fails to do justice to the phenomena it seeks to explain. This intellectual heritage is most obtrusive when psychology deals with the kinds of behavior that are least predictable in terms of species-specific survival needs: creativity, religion, and the enjoyment people derive from complex activities" (*Beyond Boredom*, 7).

11. Mihaly Csikszentmihalyi, *FLOW: The Psychology of Optimal Experience* (New York: Harper and Row, 1990), 45.

12. Csikszentmihalyi, *FLOW*, 46.

13. Csikszentmihalyi, *FLOW*, 46. When it comes to enjoyment in academic and scientific research, Csikszentmihalyi pointed out that paradoxically, research that was entered into for its own sake can sometimes end up having great usefulness. "Paradoxically,...new ideas, artifacts, and technologies of great usefulness are often discovered in activities that had no practical goals in view, but were engaged in exclusively for the enjoyment they provided." *Optimal Experience: Psychological Studies of Flow in Consciousness*, ed. Mihaly Csikszentmihalyi and Isabella Selega Csikszentmihalyi (New York: Cambridge University Press, 1988), 29.

14. Whether a particular experience of flow is leading to the growth of the person in a general sense may require reflection using broader criteria, ethical or otherwise. I will discuss this issue later in this chapter.

15. Murphy and White, *In the Zone: Transcendent Experiences in Sport* (New York: Penguin, 1995), 22.

16. Csikszentmihalyi, *FLOW*, 53–54.

17. M. Csikszentmihalyi and I. S. Csikszentmihalyi, *Optimal Experience*, 33. Csikszentmihalyi is drawing on the terminology of George Herbert Mead here. George Herbert Mead, *Mind, Self and Society*, C. W. Morris, ed. (Chicago: University of Chicago Press, 2015) original work published in 1934.

18. Csikszentmihalyi, *Beyond Boredom*, 39–40.

19. Csikszentmihalyi, *FLOW*, 64. Csikszentmihalyi explains how flow experiences are related to personal growth: "In flow a person is

challenged to do her best, and must constantly improve her skills. At the time, she doesn't have the opportunity to reflect on what this means in terms of the self—if she did allow herself to become self-conscious, the experience could not have been very deep. But afterward, when the activity is over and self-consciousness has a chance to resume, the self that the person reflects upon is not the same self that existed before the flow experience: it is now enriched by new skills and fresh achievements." Csikszentmihalyi, *FLOW*, 65–66.

20. Phil Jackson and Hugh Delehanty, *Sacred Hoops: Spiritual Lessons of a Hardwood Warrior* (New York: Hyperion, 1995), 89.

21. Mihaly Csikszentmihalyi, *The Evolving Self: A Psychology for the Third Millennium* (New York: HarperCollins, 1993), 219.

22. Csikszentmihalyi, *FLOW*, 89–90.

23. Lynne Belaief, "Meanings of the Body," *The Journal of the Philosophy of Sport* 4 (1974–1977): 59. Italics in source.

24. A person or group's *perception* of their skill level and capacity to meet a challenge is also relevant with regard to how the activity is experienced.

25. See, e.g., Mark 10:23–25, 17–25; Matt 6:19–21, 6:24; Luke 16:19–31; 12:15–21. See also, from the epistles: 1 Tim 6:10; James 5:1–6.

26. David Fleming, *Draw Me into Your Friendship, the Spiritual Exercises: A Literal Translation and Contemporary Reading of The Spiritual Exercises* (St. Louis: Institute of Jesuit Sources, 1996), 113.

27. Csikszentmihalyi, *Beyond Boredom*, 48, italics added. Phil Jackson would seem to be in agreement with Ignatius about what brings dysfunction into our lives. He points out that most players who end up in the NBA start getting special treatment already in junior high school. As they get older "they have NBA general managers, sporting goods manufacturers, and assorted hucksters *dangling money* in front of them and an entourage of agents, lawyers, friends, and family members vying for their favor. Then there's the media, which can be the most alluring temptress of all. With so many people telling them *how great they are*, it's difficult, and, in some cases, impossible, for coaches to get players to check their *inflated egos* at the gym door" (*Sacred Hoops*, 90, italics added); on this topic, see also Mihaly Csikszentmihalyi, "If We Are So Rich, Why Aren't We Happy?" *American Psychologist* 54, no. 10 (October 1999): 821–27.

Notes

28. William A. Sadler, Jr. "Play: A Basic Human Structure Involving Love and Freedom," in *Sport and the Body: A Philosophical Symposium*, ed. Ellen W. Gerber (London: Henry Kimpton Publishers, 1972), 116.

29. Sadler, "Play," 116.

30. Hugo Rahner, *Man at Play*, trans. Brian Battershaw and Edward Quinn (New York: Herder and Herder, 1967), 57–58.

31. Bob Ladouceur, "What Is a Spartan?" http://www.spartanhood.com/whatisaspartan.htm.

32. Ladouceur, "What Is a Spartan?" See also Jim Yerkovich with Patrick Kelly, *WE: A Model for Coaching and Christian Living* (Washington, DC: National Catholic Education Association, 2002). Lest we think that love is not relevant or important at elite levels of sport, it is worth noting that the most successful coach in all professional sports, basketball coach Phil Jackson, emphasizes the importance of love and compassion on a team, writing that "love is the force that ignites the spirit and binds teams together" (*Sacred Hoops*, 52).

33. Pierre Teilhard de Chardin, *The Human Phenomenon*, trans. Sarah Appleton-Weber (Portland, OR: Sussex Academic Press, 2021), 186, 187 passim.

34. Chardin, *The Human Phenomenon*, 189. Csikszentmihalyi was influenced by Chardin's thought early in his career. See, e.g., Mihaly Csikszentmihalyi, "Sociological Implications in the Thought of Teilhard de Chardin," *Zygon: Journal of Religion and Science* 5, no. 2 (June 1970): 98–186. For Csikszentmihalyi's own discussion of the relationship between differentiation and integration (union), see Karen Stansberry Beard, "Theoretically Speaking: An Interview with Mihaly Csikszentmihalyi on Flow Theory Development and Its Usefulness in Addressing Contemporary Challenges in Education," *Educational Psychology Review* 27, no. 2 (June 2015): 353–64, at 356–57.

35. Loyola, *The Spiritual Exercises and Selected Works*, ed. George E. Ganss (Mahwah, NJ: Paulist Press, 1991), 161.

36. Loyola, *Spiritual Exercises*, 164.

37. Loyola, *Spiritual Exercises*, 121.

38. Loyola, *Spiritual Exercises*, 205. The experiences associated with spiritual consolation as they are described by Ignatius have a broader reach than the flow experiences as they have been described up until now in the research. As was mentioned earlier, they can be experienced

during forgiveness and reconciliation or in the midst of suffering and loss. Perhaps in the future, researchers into the flow experience will study these dimensions of human experience as well. But the research that has already been carried out on flow experiences is immensely helpful because it provides us with a way of understanding how play and other activities, such as teaching, doing research, fixing a washing machine, painting a picture, or setting up a business plan, can have a spiritual dimension to them. In Ignatian terms, this research helps us to understand how we can find God "in all things" (Loyola, *Spiritual Exercises*, 176).

39. Gerhard Lohfink, *Jesus of Nazareth: What He Wanted, Who He Was* (Collegeville, MN: Liturgical Press, 2012).

40. Pope Francis has emphasized the centrality of joy in the Christian life, as is evident in the title of his first major document, the apostolic exhortation *Evangelii Gaudium* (The Joy of the Gospel) of November 24, 2013. See the first eight paragraphs for scripture passages having to do with joy, https://www.vatican.va/content/francesco/en/apost_exhortations/documents/papa-francesco_esortazione-ap_20131124_evangelii-gaudium.html.

41. Loyola, *Spiritual Exercises*, 207 passim.

42. According to Ignatius, growth in the Christian life depends on egolessness. As he put it in the *Spiritual Exercises*: "For everyone ought to reflect that in all spiritual matters, the more one divests oneself of self-love, self-will, and self-interests, the more progress one will make." Loyola, *Spiritual Exercises*, 166. Teilhard de Chardin's formulation may be more palatable to contemporary readers. As he put it, "The true *ego* grows in inverse ratio to "egotism." *The Human Phenomenon*, 187.

43. Beatrice Bruteau, *Radical Optimism: Practical Spirituality in an Uncertain World* (Boulder, CO: Sentient Publications, 2004), 97. Of course, while egolessness is characteristic of an experience of spiritual consolation, it can also be experienced apart from spiritual consolation.

44. Loyola, *Spiritual Exercises*, 206.

45. Address of His Holiness Pope Francis to the 36th General Congregation of the Society of Jesus, October 24, 2016, https://www.vatican.va/content/francesco/en/speeches/2016/october/documents/papa-francesco_20161024_visita-compagnia-gesu.html.

46. Thomas Aquinas, *Summa Theologica*, I–I, Q. 1, art. 8, ad 2, trans. Fathers of the English Dominican Province (New York: Benziger Brothers, 1947).

47. Peter Berger, *A Rumor of Angels: Modern Society and the Rediscovery of the Supernatural* (New York: Doubleday, 1970), 52.

CONCLUSION

1. Huizinga, *Homo Ludens*, 197, 198 passim.
2. Huizinga, *Homo Ludens*, 197–98.
3. Huizinga, *Homo Ludens*, 21.
4. Thomas Aquinas, *Summa Theologica*, I–II, Q. 1, art. 6, ad. 1, trans. Fathers of the English Dominican Province (New York: Benziger Brothers, 1947).
5. Burghardt, *The Genesis of Animal Play: Testing the Limits* (Cambridge, MA: Massachusetts Institute of Technology, 2005), 119.
6. Gerhard Lohfink, *Jesus of Nazareth: What He Wanted, Who He Was* (Collegeville, MN: Liturgical Press, 2012), 243–44.
7. Lohfink, *Jesus of Nazareth*, 244.
8. The verses above are from Psalm 65 as it appears in the Liturgy of the Hours. Italics added for emphasis.
9. Pope Francis, *Let Us Dream: The Path to a Better Future* (New York: Simon and Schuster, 2020), 80–81. The Franciscan Richard Rohr uses *flow* as the primary image to describe the Trinitarian God and the dynamics of the Christian life in his book *The Divine Dance*. Drawing on the Cappadocian Fathers, he writes that the God whom we have named Trinity is the "flow who flows through everything, without exception, and who has done so since the beginning." With regard to our living the Christian life, he writes, "The foundational good news is that creation and humanity have been drawn into this flow! We are not outsiders or spectators, but inherently part of the divine dance." Richard Rohr, with Mike Morrell, *The Divine Dance: The Trinity and Your Transformation* (New Kensington, PA: Whitaker House, 2016), 37 and 67.

INDEX

Athletes in Action, 56
autotelic, 24, 46, 58–59, 62, 65, 69, 75, 103–5, 127, 133n4

Barry, William, SJ, 89
Bellah, Robert, 15, 153n17
Benedict XVI, Pope emeritus, 86, 153n18. *See also* Ratzinger
Berger, Peter, 48
Bergmann, Fritjohf, 78–83, 85, 87, 89, 92–93, 95, 156nn22–23, 160n58
body, 52–53, 84–86, 157n38
Bruteau, Beatrice, 120
Burghardt, Gordon, 61–66, 101, 114, 127, 131, 152
Bushnell, Horace, 37–38
Buytendijk, F. J. J., 50

Campolo, Tony, 57
Chardin, Pierre Teilhard de, 116
Coakley, Jay, 4, 82
Cox, Harvey, 49
Csikszentmihalyi, Mihaly, 5, 59, 102–9, 114, 117, 118, 127, 133n4, 162n9, 163n13, 163n19

Davis, Natalie Zemon, 19–20
Descartes, René, 52, 84–85
Du Bois, W. E. B., 39

Farley, Margaret, 86, 157n38
Feezell, Randolph, 2, 5, 59, 71, 72–78, 81, 83, 88, 93, 96, 98, 127, 128
Fellowship of Christian Athletes, 56
flow: Bergmann, 80, 156n22; characteristics of activies and, 110–11; and Christian spirituality, 113–15; Csikszentmihalyi, 59, 104–5, 117, 118, 133n4, 162n9, 163n19; elements of experience of, 106–9; and ethics, 111–12; and Feezell, 128; and God, 130–31, 167n9; and Ignatius, 117–19, 121, 165n38; and Rohr, 167n9; selflessness, 108, 124, 128; and spiritual consolation, 121–24
Francis, Pope, 121, 130, 166n40

Gadamer, Hans Georg, 74, 83
Georgetown College, 30
Giamatti, A. Bartlett, 45
Gladden, Washington, 34–35
Guardini, Romano, 16, 152n3

Hale, Edward Everett, 36
Harvey, Lincoln, 57–58
Hopkins, Gerard Manley, SJ, 96–97
Huizinga, Johan, 6–16, 20, 46, 53, 71, 101, 125–26, 138n14, 139n32

Ignatius of Loyola, 72, 87–93, 113, 117–19, 121, 123, 131, 158nn45–47, 166n42
Industrial Revolution, 8

Jesuit missionaries, 28–29
Johnston, Robert, 58–59

Kerényi, Karl, 15

Ladouceur, Bob, 115–16

Market society, 9, 126
McDermott, Brian, SJ, 158n45
Meier, Klaus, 85
Merton, Thomas, 45, 94–95, 97, 160n62, 161n63
Moltmann, Jürgen, 49–50

Newman, John Henry, Cardinal, 43
Novak, Michael, 46–47, 53

Ong, Walter, SJ, 97–99
Overman, Steven, 55–56

Piccolomini, Aeneas (Pope Pius II), 26, 143n23
Pieper, Josef, 24, 43, 46
Pius XII, Pope, 26, 52–53
Plato, 15, 101
play: and freedom, 12, 15, 46, 68–69, 71–99, 114–15, 128, 154n23, 154n25; joy, 5, 11, 15, 48, 57, 76, 118–19, 124; and liturgy, 17, 45; primary process, 63–64, 66, 127; and ritual, 14–17, 125; sacred, 11–12, 14–17, 81, 125, 139n32; secondary process, 63–64, 66, 128; sport as, 1–2, 4–17, 72–77; tertiary process, 63–64, 66, 128
Puritans, 7–8, 35, 47, 55, 57, 126, 145n45, 162n6

Quenon, Paul, OCSO, 45

Rahner, Hugo, SJ, 44–45, 46, 98, 115
Ratio Studiorum, 27
Ratzinger, Josef, Cardinal, 67–70, 128, 153n18, 154n25. *See also* Benedict XVI
Rejadell, Teresa, 93

Sandel, Michael, 9
self: false, 94, 113; true, 71–72, 83, 93–97, 99, 116, 128, 160n59, 161n62

Index

spiritual consolation, 88–90, 91, 93, 118, 119, 121–23, 133n4, 158nn45–46, 159n48, 159n51, 160n58, 165n38, 166n43
spiritual desolation, 90–93, 160nn54–55, 160n58
Spiritual Exercises, 72, 87, 91, 93, 113, 118 119, 131, 160n55
Suits, Bernard, 13, 74

Taylor, Charles, 51–52
Thomas Aquinas, 21–25, 127, 142n219
Toner, Jules, SJ, 158nn45–46

University of Notre Dame, 32, 51, 144n39

Villanova University, 33